PASUNDAYAW

A Complete Handbook for Cultural Dance Research

NESTOR A. CASTAÑOS JR.

PASUNDAYAW

A Complete Handbook for Cultural Dance Research

Copyright @2021 by

Nestor A. Castaños Jr.

Published by Lulu Press Inc.

United States of America

ISBN 978-1-329-82032-6

ACKNOWLEDGMENTS

I wish to express grateful acknowledgment and thanks to those who gave their generous assistance in collecting, compiling, preparing, and finalizing the materials included in this research study.

I am especially indebted to my thesis adviser Dr. Nelson N. Enage, for the guidance and inspiration; likewise, to Dr. Sonia A. Pajaron, Chair of the panel, along with the members Dr. Rose A. Arceño, Dr. Claudine L. Igot, and Mrs. Arisa S. Pogoy for the valuable suggestions and recommendations; to Mrs. Bernley Joy M. Nobleza for editing the entire manuscript; to Mr. Aldrin A.V. Ecito and Daryll Salceda for the rondalla arrangement and notations; and the documentation team spearheaded by Mr. Myron Joshua Delgado.

I also wish to convey my thanks to the following: the DepEd Merida District Cultural performers who served as pioneering dancers; to the district supervisor, Mr. Guilermo S. Bande Jr. for allowing the researcher to test and validate the dances through teachers' performance; to the Deped Leyte Division thru the assistance of Dr. Henrietta Managbanag for letting the teachers showcase the four local folk dances during the Convergence of Education Leaders; to the Magsanga Cultural Foundation and Technical Working group for the technical assistance and supervision during their dance performance.

I am especially thankful to the local government unit of Merida through the leadership of the municipal mayor Engr. Rolando M. Villasencio for the opportunity to be part of the cultural mapping team and the cultural mappers and local historians who served as informants of the different dances.

My heartfelt appreciation to my wife - my Inspiration for her unconditional support and love for my advocacy and our family. Also, I thank relatives, co-teachers, Merida Vocational School's administration, and all my friends for their encouragement to finish the study.

Finally, I am grateful to Allah, the Divine Protector and Father of all humankind, who bestowed on me all the blessings, graces, and wisdom to finish this cultural masterpiece for so long, I had been longing and wishing for.

Nestor A. Castaños Jr.

PREFACE

PASUNDAYAW came from the corrupted visayan word "PASUNDAYAG PINAAGI SA SAYAW" which means showcasing by means of dancing. This book, PASUNDAYAW: A Complete Handbook for Cultural Dance Research, showcases the rich cultural heritage of Merida, Province of Leyte, through documentation and notations.

Folk dances have been part of Philippine culture, making the country unique and preserved through documentation. The documentation of intangible cultural heritage has been a long stand challenge within the archival community. Foreigners had written early records on Philippine dance, and true dance documentation only came in the second quarter of the 20th century, by Francisca Reyes Aquino in the late 1920s.

As dance research, this book utilized qualitative and ethnographic methods that engaged in the philosophical and socio-cultural underpinnings of Merida, Leyte's unpublished local folk dances. More so, this handbook on cultural dance research gives substantial information on how to conduct dance research for cultural preservation and aims to contribute to Aquino's pioneering works. As a method, this book adopted the Philippine Folk Dance Documentation Framework visualized by Domingo (2018) and dance analysis adopted from Cariaga's guidelines for analysis of specific movements.

TABLE OF CONTENTS

CHAPTER 1

The Roadmap in Arts Education

The road map of arts education emphasized that dance is in continuous solution and development. The lack of an accessible body of information is considered a significant setback for improving practice, influencing policymaking, and integrating the arts into educational systems. Hence, it is substantial that a current investigation on its present state is conducted.[1]

Section 14, Article XIV of the 1987 Constitution states that *"The State shall foster the preservation, enrichment and dynamic evolution of a Filipino national culture."* Section 15 mandates the state to conserve, promote, and popularized the nation's *"historical and cultural heritage and resources as well as artistic creations."* Also, in the same Article, Section 17 mandates the state to recognize, respect, and protect the rights of indigenous cultural communities to preserve and develop their cultural traditions and institutions"[2]

Furthermore, the R.A. 10066 or the "National Cultural Heritage Act of 2009" likewise mandates the state to conserve, develop, promote and popularize the nation's historical and cultural heritage and resources, as well as artistic creations.

Section 16 of the Act also mandates local government units to document traditional and contemporary arts and crafts.

Studies have also revealed that there are only a few folk dances from Leyte province and in Eastern Visayas, in general, had been gathered into a collection to perpetuate and to conserve a particular cultural art of the region for the next generation, and the next, and possibly, for posterity. The famous folk dances "Tinikling" and "Alcamfor" of the Leyteños, documented and written by Francisca-Reyes Aquino (F.R.A.), and fifteen Samareño folk dances by Juan C. Miel, were considered just a fragment of Region VIII culture, adding to the wealth of folk dances of the Philippines that have already been published and whose performances have become widely acclaimed.

Moreover, the Article X, Section 18 of the 1987 Philippine Constitution entitled Education, Science, and Technology, Arts, Culture and Sports, which states that: "(1) *The State shall ensure equal access to cultural opportunities through the educational system, public or private cultural entities, scholarships, grants, and other public venues, (2) The state shall encourage and support books and studies on the arts and culture*." Moreover, R.A. 10533 contemplates that contextualization is given emphasis and that the curriculum shall be flexible enough to its respective educational and social context.[3]

In the viewpoint of Smigel, he emphasized that reliable records of dance could further help reconstruct dances that are culturally obsolete and have been discharged from the present repertoire and confirm the need for this kind of study. Dance enthusiasts would additionally learn and understand their field's multitude of forms and styles through different documentation methods.[4]

Folk dance, perceived as being beyond change, is represented as being under threat from development. Santos puts forward the idea of Gonzalez that folk dance must be found and rescued, or it will be "drifted." Dance literature can be used to demonstrate the strengths of a comprehensive dance curriculum in addressing educational needs. The dance research agenda can include problem-solving ability, self-concept, and holistic approaches to learning. Findings of such research could help build the case for the inclusion of dance and the other arts in education.[5]

For ages past, our forefathers have been performing folk dances occasionally during social functions, and young people have been dancing them during town and barrio fiestas to entertain the people. In the wake of diverse contemporary entertainment, it is apparent that these folk dances are gradually but surely being forgotten and, like the tamaraw, are on the verge of extinction.

According to Antonio Jr. of the National Commission For Culture and the Arts, it is essential to consider cultural mapping and resource profiling as one of the systematic approaches in identifying, recording, and classifying all existing cultural properties or resources of a particular community to document, describe, visualize, and understand them. Many of its benefits can be realized through sustained efforts in generating and updating cultural databases over time.[6]

Cultural mapping is a process to identify and document the cultural resources or assets of a community. Across the country, more and more communities turn to cultural mapping as an important new tool to support economic development and enrich the community's quality of life.

From September 2 to October 5, 2019, Merida, province of Leyte, partnered with DepEd Merida District, conducted a cultural mapping activity. Cultural heritage (both tangible and intangible) was uncovered and discovered that served as a basis for further artistic development and preservation projects.

Local folk dances were identified and considered the undiscovered and undocumented treasures of Merida. These local folk dances include "Ang Kutsero," "Binaylehan," "Jota Merida," and "Pamabhas." The entertainment evolved-dance "Ang Kutsero" is performed by men as "kutsero" and women as "pasahero." The "Binaylehan" is a courtship or entertainment dance in which barrio folks have a notable version of the close-hold position while dancing. The Spanish-influenced dance "Jota Merida" is a localized version of the Spanish jota of Merida, Spain. "Pamabhas" is a mimetic or entertainment dance commonly performed among villagers during a bountiful catch of fish and when the full moon occurs. These local dances need to have continuous research since they must be recorded and preserved, not to be left in antiquity.

CHAPTER 2

Evolution of Philippine Cultural Dance

The Philippines is a growing nation, ready to transcend barriers for expansion, and the world has suddenly become smaller; separated people in the past have given way to what is now known as "world culture." Dance is one of the potent factors in the improvement, promotion, or strengthening of tradition. Traditional dances still reflect traditions, customs, and religious beliefs retained in a near-pristine form that could offer a valuable club in today's search for authentic roots of pre-Hispanic Philippines[1].

Since the earliest times, all people in the world have dances. Anthropologists and dance historians have surmised that early man may have learned to dance from watching birds and animals as they performed courting rituals and other dance-like movements. Early dance comes from rock and cave paintings from the dance of primitive societies still in existence. While the exact details of how and why man began to dance are unknown, there is a reason to believe it was one of man's greatest preoccupations. For all significant life activities, the man used dance rituals.[2]

According to Alejandro, dance was a vital means of social communication and celebrated significant life events such as birth, birthdays, courtships, funerals, harvests, and victorious warriors' return or hunters. In supplication, the man danced to induce the gods to be benignly disposed to every event in life. Children learned history and the mores of the tribe through dance. Traditional dance reflects traditions, customs, and religious beliefs retained in a near-pristine form that could offer a valuable club in today's search for the pre-Hispanic Philippines' authentic roots. [2]

Moreover, the Folk (traditional) dances are a sequence of movement formations and rhythmic patterns created by people of different cultures. This dance is native and evolved instinctively and spontaneously. It is communal in purpose and unique and predicated upon the principle of group participation. Values are derived from folk dancing. It provides knowledge and information on other people's folklore, superstition, legends, rituals, customs, celebrations, and festivals.

In the book of Alejandro, he noted that there are traditional dances, especially those imitating living creatures like animals and plants. People also created dances from rituals and incantations of shamans to their gods or spirits for good harvests, success in war, and cures for the sick. There are also many occupational and life cycle ritual dances for birth, death, courtship, and marriage. They patterned their movements from the traditional practices that their great forefathers did, like ritual dramas that tell stories and legends that were essential parts of their cultural history. People have used dance to express their cultural elements as far back as the human race can be traced. The dance is the showcase of the way of life of the people in the society.[3]

Besides, the Philippine folk dance has moved from participatory cultural activity to object of study, integration into performance practice by large folk-dance companies (such as Bayanihan), and "neo-ethnic" performance practice. Dance not only has been the subject of interpretation and reinterpretation by academics, but it has also become an instrument for research.[4]

In case author Ceasar Nimor, author of Unpublished Folk Dances of Cebu Province for Choreography and Production, once said: *"Culture is what sets man apart from the rest of Kingdom Animalia and that the best expression of culture is through folk dancing."* Janson also believes that *"The more we learn about our cultural heritage, the more powerful our reasons for cooperating with and respecting each other as one people."* Folk dance is a good vehicle for preserving and showcasing our culture. Folk dances are a sequence of movement formation and rhythmic patterns that people of different cultures have created.[5]

As per Werbner, Philippine folk (traditional) dance is a national form of dance presentation. A variety of local dances are brought together into a program and presented through the medium of theater. The use of the concept of two forms of hybridization, distinguished by Bakhtin, the Philippine folk dance is characterized by the combination of both "organic" and "intentional" hybridization.[6]

From a perspective of a certain specialist, the organic unconscious hybridity is a historical phenomenon that "evolves culture historically through unreflexive borrowings, mimetic appropriation, trade, and inventions," it does not disturb the sense of continuity. In contrast, intentional or conscious hybridity "shocks, alters, threatens, revitalizes, or disrupts through deliberate, planned fusions."

Santos contended the Philippine folk dance idea, which represents Western and Asian cultural elements visible in local dance traditions, brings the country's colonial past to the fore. Although claimed to be unique "ours" or "Filipino" and not something just borrowed from the West, the Christian-Filipino representations of folk dance are unique in Southeast Asia. The age-old classical or court dances of many other Southeast Asian countries are presented as national and worthy of preservation. They do not show any trace or evidence of colonial past[6]

At long last, according to Reyes, the Filipinos were born dancers and musicians. Through dance, the individuals and the community's lives reflect the human spirit's most profound sensitivities. Due to this inclination, Philippine folk dances became part of the schools' physical education program in 1915. Dance is part of our culture, and it helps preserve social customs and traditions by passing them along from one generation to another.[7]

Another viewpoint upheld the idea that the Philippine folk dances are as old as the history itself, which is rarely seen at present. In the Philippines, most people believe that culture depicts dancing as part of customs and traditions, modes of expression, leisure activity, entertainment, and profession. Folk dance still exists in all the forms described and is a self-reflective tool in their investigation of cultural practices.[1]

Mrs. Francisca-Reyes Aquino Tolentino was the first Filipino woman to be sent to the United States to specialize in Physical Education, making a major contribution to Physical Education. Her book studies are focused on Philippine folk dance, writing them in book form to nationalize and spread them through making them available to field teachers and training leaders for dissemination. According to Aquino, as quoted by Cariaga, factors that influence folk dances are:

1. **Customs and Traditions**. As a people, the Filipinos, especially the past women, are shy, sensitive, modest, slow, and reserved. These traits are found in many of our dances. In courtship dances, girls do not accept their favored suitors readily or immediately. They always say "No" while their feelings mean "Yes." The shaking of hands in "Pandang-Pandang" is very different from how we greet each other at present. The custom in the old days for the women to offer only two fingers (the second and the third) shook hands.

2. **Climate Environment**. This factor has a significant influence on the nature of the dances of any nation. We can quickly say that dances came from the cold regions if the dance has vigorous, passionate, and energetic steps. They abound by skips, jumps, leaps, hops, springs, turns, and running steps. The movements are suitable for the climatic conditions. In a tropical climate, dances are generally slow, languorous, and energetic. Tropical countries like ours typically have slow, languorous, weird, and dreamy dances. In the Philippines, most dances belong to the slow and moderate type, although we have some fast and energetic ones like the "Tinikling," the "Sakuting," the "Maglalatik," and the war dances of the non-christian. Speedy and vigorous dances are too strenuous and fatiguing in our climatic conditions.

3. **Economic conditions**. In areas where life is easy, the dances are gay and lively. On the other hand, where life is

hard, dances are slow, sad, and mournful. The music and songs of different places vary in the same way.[1]

More so, the nature of folk dance, according to Reyes, includes the following:

1. Occupational Dance - depicts actions of a particular occupation
2. Religious/Ceremonial Dance - associated with religion, vows, and ceremonies
3. Comic/Mimetic Dance - shows funny movements for entertainment and imitates movements of birds, animals, etc.
4. Game Dance - done with play elements
5. Wedding Dance - performed during wedding feasts
6. Courtship Dance - depicts the art of courtship
7. Festival/Entertainment Dance - suitable for special occasions
8. War Dance - show imagery combat.

The study of folk dancing gives an informational background on the Filipino people's history to better understand and appreciate its political and religious origin. Folk dances must be promoted, propagated, and preserved for future generations. Every physical education teacher's responsibility is to teach folk dances with dedication and commitment to increase and maintain them.[8]

CHAPTER 3

The Challenge of Documenting Intangible Cultural Dance Heritage

The documentation of intangible cultural heritage has been a longstanding challenge within the archival community. In its 2003 Convention, UNESCO describes intangible cultural heritage as "traditions or living expressions inherited from our ancestors and passed on to our descendants, such as oral traditions, performing arts, social practices, rituals, festive events, knowledge, and practices concerning nature and the universe or the knowledge and skills to produce traditional craft." Furthermore, the UNESCO Convention stated, "The importance of intangible cultural heritage is not the cultural manifestation itself but rather the wealth of knowledge and skills that is transmitted through it from one generation to the next."

Intangible cultural heritage is evolutionary because the practices are passed from person to person and generationally change according to the community's natural circumstances. As a result, each heritage feature chosen for preservation has a documentation plan customized to the community's needs and traditions. Since UNESCO's first selections for conservation in 2008, over 500 intangible cultural heritage practices have been targeted for safeguarding and documentation; 180 of these selections are cultural dances, mostly from developing countries. Very few western cultural elements have been selected for safeguarding, especially within the dance field. Instead, Western dance documentation on all libraries and artistic book institutions, but challenges arise when organizations face archiving materials that require substantial interpretation and institutional knowledge.[1]

According to the Dance Heritage Coalition, dance is the highest form of art, as Domingo cited. However, it receives the least number of book outputs merely because of the lack of resources (dance literature) and very few individuals who passionately want to do book and documentation. It was further noted that "with good record-keeping of the role of dance in art and culture, scholars can better develop both the theory and the criticism that will ensure dance's place in the academe." Through dance notation, dances can be well-preserved and be passed on from generation to generation.[2]

At long last, dance is considered part of one's personal and cultural experience, and its past, present, and future deserve to be safeguarded. The purpose of documentation is to provide access to that experience over time. The tools that can fully document such a three-dimensional form have not been available until this century. Although these resources have developed and continue to grow, there is now the potential to participate in significant documentation, take on the preservation challenge, and concentrate on how the documentation tools are used.

Furthermore, the Dance Heritage Coalition, Inc. cited three important components of dance documentation: (1) representing the process, (2) representing the performance event, and (3) representing the cultural impact. If these three aspects of the dance event can be preserved and examined, people looking back will have enough information to evaluate its significance and cultural impact. Giving forethought to dance documentation contributes to recognizing and identifying essential dance and dance studies. Nevertheless, dance documentation serves different needs and uses, for both the long and the short term. A dance's documentation ensures students, scholars, cultural commentators, and others for performance, study, and analysis in the bigger picture. Some methods of documentation enable a dance to be reproduced in future times and contexts. In the short term, documentation may serve as a tool for audience-building, publicity, grant applications, rehearsal aids, and other uses. The long-term benefits of dance documentation are often not seriously considered by practicing dance communities for economics, time, and resources.[3]

An exploration of the Dance notation used scores function like music scores: they provide a stable written record based on codified symbols that can be used later to recreate or study the work. Various dance notation systems provided the first conscientious technique for documenting dance. They are primarily used to fix a dance's form and style by creating a written record through notation results in an intentional and highly accurate documentation product.

Labanotation or Kinetography Laban is a notation system for recording and analyzing human movement derived from Rudolf Laban's work, who described it in Schrifttanz

("Written Dance") 1928. Labanotation uses abstract symbols to define the (1) direction and level of the movement, (2) part of the body doing the movement, (3) duration of the movement, (4) dynamic quality of the movement, and (5) direction and level of the movement. The shapes of the direction symbols indicate nine different directions in space, and the symbol's shading specifies the movement's level. Each "direction symbol" indicates the orientation of a line between the proximal and distal points of a body part or a limb; that is, "the direction signs indicate the direction towards which the limbs must incline." The direction symbols are organized into three levels: high, middle, and low or deep.[4]

Benesh Movement Notation (B.M.N.), also known as Benesh notation or choreology, is a dance notation system used to document dance and other types of human movement. Invented by Joan and Rudolf Benesh in the late 1940s, the system uses abstract symbols based on symbolic representations of the human body. It is used in choreography and physical therapy and by the Royal Academy of Dance to teach ballet. Benesh notation is recorded on a five-line staff from left to right, with vertical bar lines to mark the passage of time. Because of its similarity to modern staff music notation, Benesh notation can be displayed alongside (typically below) and synchronized with musical accompaniment.[5]

Eshkol-Wachman (EWMN) movement notation is a notation system for recording movement on paper or computer screens. Eshkol-Wachman (EWMN) is a dance notation system created in Israel by dance theorists Noa Eshkol (1924–2007) and Abraham Wachman (1931–2010). Eshkol-Wachman movement notation treats the body as a sort of stick figure. The body is divided at its skeletal joints, and each pair of joints defines a line segment (a "limb"). For example, the foot is a limb bounded by the ankle and the end of the toe. The system is used in many fields, including dance, physical therapy, animal behavior, and early diagnosis of autism[6].

The Aquino's way of notating and documenting traditional and folk dances became mainstream among Philippine folk dance authors. She influenced the direction of folk dance took through her methods of investigation, collection, and inscription. Dances were recorded and to include the title, dance culture, the place of origin, ethnolinguistic group and classification, the costumes and the props, the music, the musical instruments used, and the instruction of the dance, which includes the figures with respective dance steps and movements, counts and number of measures. She made her own decisions concerning what could be considered folk dance, how much could be altered and for what reasons, and how her choreographic work would fit into the developing canon. Aquino took her choreographed dances, supported by her ethnographic book and critical reflection, and placed them in the Filipino folk dance canon.[7]

The use of movement has primarily been confined to Aquino's verbal and directional system, arranged into figures and fitted into counts and phrases. Larry Gabao teaches Labanotation at the Philippine Normal University, and Villaruz teaches the Benesh system at the University of the Philippines. These more developed systems have not been widely accepted for lack of tutors and passivity among dance teachers. Two organizations in folk dance that seek to safeguard dance traditions are the Philippine Folk Dance Society and the Francisca Reyes Aquino Memorial Foundation. In theatrical dance, there are too few authors.

Oral history has been collected by the dance program at the UP College of Music and a few more by Marcelino Foronda. Among the early writers on Philippine theater are Vicente Barrantes (1889), Juan Atayde (1892), and Wenceslao Retana (1909), and comprehensively surveyed up to 1946 by Cristina Laconico Buenaventura (1994). In the '70s and '80s, the Ballet Federation of the Philippines published its newsletter Sayaw Silanganan (edited by Villaruz) and Ballet Philippines its Dance Philippines (edited by Nestor Jardin). Villaruz and Jardin have contributed to several foreign publications on the subject of Philippine dance. Leonor Orosa Goquingco has contributed to Enciclopedia dello Spettacolo and Grove's Dictionary of Music and Musicians, and Reynaldo Alejandro to International Dance Encyclopedia.[8]

The study of Luna cited that although textual, Filipino folk-dance publication in the last two decades has become more anthropological and uses a more holistic approach with a book team involved in writing singular viewer's dance. Three volumes of them were by Libertad Fajardo. Urtula's P.W.U. Co-faculty, who helped stage the folk dance recitals, authored a book on Visayan dances. The study included the pronunciation of the dance title, notation of steps and formation in words, grade placement for each dance, a one-sentence history of the dance, the name of the informant, costume description in the text, photos of costumes at the start of the book and musical notation. These published books about folk dance for primary and secondary education also adopted F.R.A methods of dance notation.[9]

Also, according to Villaruz, for the most part, early records on Philippine dance had been written by foreigners;

among the most notable ones are Antonio Pigafetta (Ferdinand Magellan's historian), Fr. Francisco Colin, and Jean Mallat. Correct documentation of dance only came in the second quarter of the 20th century, by Francisca Reyes Aquino in the late 1920s when she worked on her thesis and further went out to the field with Ramon Tolentino and Antonio Buenaventura as a team under the auspices of the University of the Philippines president, Jorge Bocobo. These also resulted in the UP Folk Song and Dance Club that toured the provinces and the publication of Philippine Folk Dances and Games (1935) with Petrona Ramos and Philippine National Dances (1946). Aquino further extended her book and publication through the years, the most outstanding of the six-volume Philippine Folk Dances (1953 – 1979). She was assisted by some other authors like Emerita Basilio in Luzon and Jose Balcena in the Visayas.[8]

Emulating F.R.A's example, others followed with their regional authors: like Libertad V. Fajardo with three volumes on Visayan dances (1961 – 1975); Juan C. Miel on Samar dances (1973); Jovita Sison Friese on Pangasinan dances (1980); Teresita Pascua Ines on Ilocano dances; Petronila Suarez on Iloilo dances; Lourdes Buena and Leon Tuy on Bicol songs and dances; Gloria Cabahug on Cebuano dances; and coordinated book on Antique dances led by Abelardo Villavert. Ramon Obusan also had the most extensive collection of video films on Philippine dances, with several of them used in the Cultural Center of the Philippines-produced the Tuklas Sining series on the arts. Two of the four video documentations on dance directed by Obusan and scripted by Basilio Esteban S. Villaruz have won national and international awards.

Johnson and Snyder (Securing Our Dance Heritage: Issues in the Documentation and Preservation of Dance) highlighted the opportunity to engage in significant documentation, take on the challenge of preservation, and focus on how the documentation tools are used. Visual and written documentation provides fragmented glimpses of the presence and significance of dance throughout humankind's history.

The reality is that dance is multidimensional, perhaps the most complex of all expressive forms. Dance is part of our personal and cultural experience, and its past, present, and future deserve to be safeguarded. The evolution from simple verbal descriptions to more multidimensional "bird's eye views" made the literature more plausible. Before the Renaissance period, dance played a significant role in Western European societies.

Dance documentation books in the American period combined symbols, signs, pictures, and word descriptions which were the first to present dance from a multidimensional perspective. Hence, they were the first to have a specific demonstration on documenting and preserving the dance and advancing toward overcoming the time/space dichotomy. Still, photography came into being in the mid-nineteenth century. Soon the photograph was considered capable of capturing "reality," but it was still a two-dimensional medium, another stepping stone on the way to more accurate documentation. The Dance Heritage Coalition (D.H.C.) member institutions are grappling with these very issues and, in so doing, are setting high standards for documenting and preserving the performing arts and other events that take place in time and space. It is often said that dance is brief and therefore eludes documentation.[10]

The growth of electronic media in the 1990s brought the new potential for the documentation and preservation of dance and access to dance materials. Electronic media embrace the computer's capabilities and such forms as CD-ROM, DVD, and other telecommunications' emerging tools. Over the last 15 years, videotape has developed into a crucial tool for recording dance and has become a form of currency in the dance community.

As the late dance videographer Michael Schwartz wrote in the Poor Dancer's Almanac: "Of all the arts, dance has been the most profoundly affected by the widespread use of video technology. Choreographers, dancers, critics, historians, and producers now have a tool that can preserve the ephemeral material of rehearsal and performance - for repeated, detailed viewing. Video has affected not only the preservation and teaching of established repertory but also the work process itself. Instant replay allows the dancer and choreographer to rework and edit a dance as it evolves, edited into promotional tapes. Video documentation has become an essential part of the business of all performance - a tool required by funders and presenters to determine who receives funding and who is presented".[11]

The recording of the dance and music culture can be considered the first phase in the ethnographic research and documentation of traditional folk dances. Dance ethnography analyzes the movement systems created in the context of a geographical and historical process and ethnic structure to understand society's cultural structure. Dance ethnology aims to understand society and its culture via dance analysis. Together with dance ethnology that tries to understand dance via society, these have become a two-disciplined field of study combined under the branch of ethnochoreology.[12]

Ethnochoreology (also dance ethnology, dance anthropology) is studying dance by applying some disciplines such as anthropology, musicology, ethnomusicology, and ethnography. Accompanying the trend toward dance ethnography is the discussion of subdisciplines under dance literature. Iyer differentiates dance iconography from dance anthropology, analyzing movement systems of societies that generated living dance traditions. Her forte, dance iconography, studies documented dance poses to present movement phase, movement cadence, or stance rather than static positions. She also explains that dance history's concern is more on the evolution and development of particular forms.[13]

In an ethnographic-phenomenological type of inquiry and observation, as revealed in Enage's study, understanding various actual and historical facts and motivations are a few things to be considered in the dance research. Results showed that emerging themes were developed, such as the creative process, the music, the props, the choreography, and the costume design. Understanding the origin and the observation of an actual setting greatly helped create the dance. The creative process helped realize the root of history through dance taken from the artifacts showing the participants' religion and livelihood.[14]

Logically, interdisciplinary studies are relevant to folk dance literature and communicate her strife to intersect anthropology, indigenous studies, dance studies, and African studies. Thus, examining dance in an ethnographic manner is to perceive it "in the contextual web of social relationships, environment, religion, aesthetics, politics, economy, and history.

In retrospect, folk dance authors can reveal patterns in Philippine folk dance literature and publication. In doing so, the dance book community can significantly advance how they study dances. In his dance study on approaching dance, Luna shared common ideas with Giurchescu and Torp, urging other dance authors to support the dance research book as it is a "necessary instrument" in revealing the "dance process," its constituents, their meanings, and functions in the society. They expound that knowing these helps people understand their means of expression within the "framework of socio-cultural community." Besides, they claimed that dance iconography provides only additional information but is out of the movement context. They encourage recording full dance textures using film, videotapes, and occasionally in pencil notes for field research. [13]

The traditional dance can be identified generally as a physical and emotional behavior created due to the individual's creativity in the movement system with aesthetic and rhythmic meanings common in society. The dance contains individual physical, psychological, and mental qualities and social, historical, and environmental factors. Dance analysis is made in terms of structural movement system (body and movement concepts), profound and superficial structures (cultural philosophy), social (ethnic and cultural identity), motif and choreography (as language analogies and components), local genre categories, ethnohistory (icons, historical writings, oral history), teaching methods and learning, composition, and improvisation.[15]

From this respect, to record traditional dance as an ethnographic value, one has to identify the significance of the "dance event" where the movements are used symbolically and focus on "dance performance" that occurs via the conscious awareness of the body. The dance and music culture recording can be considered the first phase in the ethnographic studies of traditional folk dances production. For the ethnographical dance recordings to be successful, it is essential to identify the cultural perceptions of the traditional dance culture that members created in their consciousness. The field book consisting of the basis of the dance ethnography contains reality. [16]

In the Philippines, the folk (traditional) dance began to be collected from the late 1920s by Francisca Reyes Aquino, known before her second marriage as Francisca Reyes Tolentino. Filipino folk dance expert Ramon P. Santos points out that the ideas of fixing and standardizing forms (such as through notation) are "western" based. As she started collecting folk dance in the Philippines in the 1920s, a development described in one authoritative source is as follows: "Realizing that with the further impact of Western culture, many of these indigenous dances would be lost or extensively modified." This quote, and the rest of the introduction, illustrates a model elaborated and discussed by John Storey in *Inventing Popular Culture: From Folklore to Globalization* in 2003.[17]

In his book findings, Declan addresses authors Francisca Reyes Aquino, Sally Ann Ness, and Benildanze, who use embodied practices to study Filipino folk dance in the academy divergent methodologies. Aquino uses ethnography, Ness phenomenology, and Benildanze practices as a book. It examines the process by which dances have moved from functioning rituals to representative artifacts and book tools.

These processes reveal a complex and constantly developing relationship between dance practice and the academy. While all three have demonstrated embodied book methods, book aims were driven by different imperatives, ranging from the desire to "save" the dances and preserve them through inscription, which shows an enormous change in the perception of the functions the dance can perform and can be made to perform, from rewriting history. While organizations such as the Philippine Folk Dance Society exist to preserve the dances, perhaps the continuing role of academia is to explore how the dances can generate knowledge in other ways. [18]

The author shared the same sentiments with Luna, Villaruz, and the other folk dance authors in the Philippines, inspired by the pioneering works of Francisca Reyes Aquino's way of dance notation and documentation. As a major component of the fitness and values revitalization program of DepEd, it has one of its objectives to identify, document, and institutionalized the traditional songs and dances to enrich the present curricula at all levels.

In the view of the applied and related studies above, dance enthusiasts would learn and understand their field's multitude of forms and styles through its different documentation methods and autochthonous practice. For dance authorities, scholars, performing artists, enthusiasts, teachers, and students, with a deep appreciation for the promotion and preservation of the rich Philippine folk dances, dance documentation is a form of retrieval to take one step towards understanding the window to the complex history of the Philippines showcasing customs, culture, and traditions.[3]

CHAPTER 4

The Philippine Folk Dance Documentation Framework
(By John Paul Domingo)

ETHICAL CONSIDERATION	• (a.) Prior knowledge; (b.) Source; (c.) Permit and approval; (d.) Study of published and unpublished dances; and (e.) Social recognition
METHODOLOGY	• (a.) Immersion; (b.) Participation; (c.) Communication; (d.) Analysis of related literature; and (e.) Field notes, memo and journal
ACTUAL DANCE DOCUMENTATION	• (a.) Context; (b.) Use of technology; (c.) Dance elements; (d.) Movement transcription; and (e.) Notation (Universal)
EVALUATION	• (a.) Narratives; (b.) Documentation evidence's; (c.) Dance presentation; (d.) Annotation; and (e.) Revalidation by source, authorities and experts
OUTPUT	• (a.) Qualitative research and study; (b.) Media utilization; (c.) Education and community programs; (d.) Staging; and (e.) Special trainings and instructions

To illuminate and guide a cultural dance researcher, one must anchor to the study of Domingo (2018), which revealed that the folk dance documentation practices in the Philippines involve ethical consideration, methodology, actual dance documentation, evaluation, and output. The Philippine Folk Dance Documentation Framework sought answers from dance authorities connected with the National Commission for Culture and the Arts (NCCA), Cultural Center of the Philippines (C.C.P.), Philippine Folk Dance Society (PFDS), leading folk dance companies in the Philippines such as the Philippine Barangay Folk Dance Troupe (PBFDT) and Ramon Obusan Folkloric Group (ROFG), curriculum experts of Department of Education (DepEd) and Commission on Higher Education (CHED), and other informants with relevant experiences in Philippine folk dance documentation.

The **ethical consideration** relates to the significant elements that must be secured before fieldwork of folk dance documentation. In this core category, the researcher must first know local folk dances and the key informants who can give factual information about the dances. Permits and approval from them are necessary to ensure that the research is conducted responsibly and ethically accountable, leading to beneficial outcomes. Similar published and unpublished studies were used as a model in the documentation process. The Municipal mayor's identification (I.D) Card duly signed was worn to earn social recognition as a cultural mapper.

The **methodology** is the core category name given to the significant concepts in this group classification. This implies the various ways of folk dance documentation in general. With this, to get essential ideas about local folk dances, the researcher immersed, participated, and conversed with the key informants. In data gathering, the researcher documented the information using field notes, memos, and journals. The gathered information on the local folk dances was analyzed according to specific movement analysis guidelines.

Actual dance documentation is defined here as the utilization of specific tools necessary for folk dance documentation. The researcher conceptualized the local dances based on the key informants' context through technology (video recording tool), dance elements, and movement transcription in this core category. The researcher adopted the F.R.A. dance notation system.

Evaluation is defined as the validation process of emerged dance documentation tools. In this core category, a dance showcasing local dances shall be mounted to validate whether the dance is acceptable to the local community. Revalidation by source, authorities, and experts was made for evaluation purposes. Annotations were properly documented and recorded for refinement.

The **output** is a core category title given to transforming or disseminating the documented folk dance outcomes. In this study, the main output is to develop dance literature to preserve the local cultural heritage of the place, particularly on their local folk dances. Conducting special training and instructions and staging the local dances using the final dance literature helped disseminate the local folk dances to the local community.

CHAPTER 5
The Visual Model on Cultural Dance Research
(By Nestor A. Castaños Jr.)

PHASE 3

PHASE 2

PHASE 1

Cultural Mapping

Philosophical Perspectives of Local Folk Dances

Four Local Folk Dances of Merida Leyte

Dance Literature (Four Local Folk Dances of Merida Leyte)

The Philippine Folk Dance Documentation Framework

Histo-Cultural Perspectives of Local Folk Dances

In qualitative research, a dance researcher must undergo different phases of data processes and analyses. The Visual Model on Study Framework presented the overall framework on how the local folk dances of Merida were being researched.

Phase 1 documented the four local folk dances as an output of Merida Leyte's cultural mapping activity. It adopted the Philippine Folk Dance Documentation Framework. This represented an informal collection of dances by which informants were carefully selected based on their knowledge about local folk dances in the local community through multiple types of gathering information. Observations and field notes on the content of their stories or narration are essential in this phase.

Phase 2 of the study analyzed the documented local folk dances as to their perspectives according to their philosophical and histo-cultural underpinnings. The informants' stories were analyzed and then retold into a framework that makes sense— retelling the process of reorganizing the stories into some general framework. This framework is consists of gathering stories, analyzing them for the elements, and rewriting the stories to place them within the organizational sequence. One aspect of chronology is that the narration has a beginning, middle, and end. The storyline includes information about the setting or context of the local folk dances. Beyond the chronology, detailed themes may be discovered to provide a more detailed discussion about dances. In the end, the narrative study tells the story of the local folk dances to unfold in chronology and including the important themes in their lives experience. Narrative inquiries are stories lived and told (Clandin, 2000). Cariaga's guidelines for analyzing specific movements portraying character traits and customs depicted in a folk dance will complete the chronology.

Phase 3 focused on the creation of dance literature based on the results of Phase 2. The dance literature of Merida's four local folk dances is the core output of this study, which was then a good material for preserving the intangible cultural heritage of the Meridanons and for future generations to come.

A Visual Model on Study Framework was developed to guide the researcher for data analysis. This presents the overall process or flow of how the study was conducted. Phase 1 documented the four local folk dances that served as the municipality's outcome of Merida, Leyte's cultural mapping activity, adopting the Philippine Folk Dance Documentation Framework. Phase 2 of the study analyzed the documented local folk dances and their perspectives under philosophical and histo-cultural underpinnings. Phase 3 focused on the creation of dance literature based on the results of Phase 2.

As dance research, this study used qualitative and ethnographic method to engage in the philosophical and socio-cultural underpinnings of Merida's different local folk dances, Leyte. This study ends given developing dance literature for cultural preservation and bringing it to the new generation. As ethnographic research, questions and observations generally relate to social and cultural processes and shared meanings of the local folk dances of Meridanons. Traditionally, this is associated with long-term fieldwork, but some aspects are employed in applied settings. As a method, this study adopted the Philippine Folk Dance Documentation Framework visualized by Domingo. Movement and dance analysis were done adopting F.R.A.'s standard practices of transcribing and notating dance movements to develop dance literature.

The researcher intended to examine the philosophical basis of the local folk dances through ontology, epistemology,

31

axiology, and methodology. This philosophical stance is required in conducting the study to provide grounding on the perceptual perspective on what to look for and how methodologically to describe the events in this study. The reality was seen as multiple and subjective constructed by individuals. Quotes and themes in the informants' words were reported to provide evidence of different prospective (Valencia, 2014).

Ontologically, this sought to determine the underlying reality, nature, beliefs, culture, and traditions as lived by Meridanons, considering the physical, emotional, and cultural appeal as reflected in the dance movements.

Epistemologically, this sought to determine the relationship between the researcher and what will be studied. Knowledge of the dance can be acquired through personal experience as expressed by the locales and gathering data through the collection of their stories. The narrative analysis was employed as a data source to generate an enormous cultural meaning to their local dances. These were done through an in-depth interview by the researcher and the informants. The researcher also observed the different movements, dance positions, and formations. The researcher observed and interacted with the informants to gather all the necessary information and minimize the distance between himself and the research subject. Utilizing fieldwork, the researcher collaborated and spent time in fields with the participants.

From an axiological perspective, the dance movement was then analyzed according to the underlying values, emotions, expressions, ethics, and aesthetics, which were part of the notation of the local folk dances. The study sought to answer a question on the role of values in the inquiry and assume that subjective values are inevitable, desirable, and value-laden. Personal interpretation of the local folk dances was reported in conjunction with informants' understanding. This is termed positioning, where the values are openly discussed, and biases were presented and acknowledged.

Methodologically, in observing the rhetoric assumption, the language utilized is personal and engaging. The data gathered during the cultural mapping activity was chronologically arranged and sequenced from the key informants. Subjectivity might occur since the researcher had insider knowledge of the local dances. Along the documentation process, non-quantifiable qualities became an object for subjectivity, such as the dance's emotional appeal.

Specific guidelines were adopted to avoid subjectivity and evolving interpretations dominating the method, particularly in analyzing movements. Since this study is field research, the researcher used opportunistic or emergent sampling that is flexible and made sampling decisions while collecting data.

As the researcher gained more knowledge on Meridanons' local dances as the informants unfold, the researcher made sampling decisions that took advantage. Flexible research and sampling design are essential qualitative research features, particularly when the research is exploratory. When little is known about a phenomenon or set, a priori sampling decisions can be difficult. Creating a research design that is flexible enough to foster reflection, preliminary analysis, and opportunistic or emergent sampling may be a good idea in such circumstances. This would indeed result in a more context-bounded or contextualized research outcome. The analyzed dance movements were written in a narrative presentation with qualification analysis that seeks understanding, especially on the movement patterns, to develop dance literature.

The four local folk dances identified during the cultural mapping of the municipality of Merida served as the instrument of study. The Philippine Folk Dance Documentation Framework was used as a general procedure guide for data gathering. Emulating most of the country's folk dance researchers, this study adopted Francisca Reyes Aquino's (F.R.A.'s) documentary analysis method, which is confined to the verbal and directional system arranged into figures and fitted into counts and phrases. The researcher, for this reason, adopted F.R.A's standards in dance notation since still more of the developed systems like Labanotation and Benesh have not been widely accepted for lack of tutors and passivity among dance teachers (Villaruz B. E., 2020).

CHAPTER 6
Ang Kutsero

Meaning: A person who drives/manages a horse-drawn carriage known in Cebuano term as "Tartanilya."

Dance Culture: Christian Lowland (town)

Place of Origin: Merida Leyte

Ethno Linguistic Group: Cebuano/Bisaya

Classification/Nature: Festival/Entertainment

Background / Content:

The Tartanilya, also known as "calesa" in Tagalog, is the most predominant transportation mode during the Spanish colonization in the Philippines. It is a Cebuano term for a horse-drawn carriage that a "Kutsero manages." Spanish occupation in the town is also evident because of the existence of the Hacienda de Martinez, now known as JOSAN FARM, which according to the old folks, plenty of horses were managed and raised by the Martinez and were used as a mode of transportation in their hacienda in the olden times.

Men perform this dance as "kutsero" and women as "pasahero." In this dance, the "pasahero" will be bringing with her a fan while waiting for the Tartanilya to pass on the street so that she can ride on it. The dancers imitated steps/movements of the horse through galloping to show how lovely is the dance. This dance depicts Meridanons' sweet, loving and happy cultural traits before and even in modern times. The Tartanilya may not be grown in numbers, but it never goes out of sight through this dance.

Dance Properties:
    Costume:

Male:	Camisa de Chino or Barong Tagalog and Dark- colored pants
Top:	Camisa de Chino/Barong Tagalog worn over a kamiseta (undershirt)
Pants: karsones (pants)	Dark-colored
Accessories:	Leather brimmed hat with colored tassel trimmings
Footwear: shoes)	Sapatos (leather
Female:	Old Balintawak and a soft pañuelo over L shoulder.
Tapis:	any printed tapis
Props:	paypay (big fan)
Footwear:	Sapatilya

Costume Illustration:

Diagram A (Starting Formation):

> Three or four pairs are arranged at the left side of the stage, and the others are arranged at the right side of the stage

O   O   O   O   Stage   O   O   O   O

※ ※ ※ ※   ※ ※ ※ ※

Audience

Note :   O - Girl
         ※ - Boy

Diagram A

Music: 2 / 4 composed of six parts: A, B, C, D, E, and F

Count: One, two, one and two, or one and two and to a measure

Basic Steps:

1. MARTSA KUTSERO (1). Starting with R foot, take four stamps with R and L foot alternately (cts.1,2,1,2). The Boy holds the hat at the top with R hand and raises the hat overhead every first count of the measure. Freehand (L hand) on the rear at waist level .... **(2M)**

2. MARTSA PASAHERO (1). Starting with R foot, take four stamps with R and L foot alternately (cts.1,2,1,2). The Girl holds the fan with R hand in front in fanning movement at chest level. Freehand (L hand) holding skirt .... **(2M)**

3. MARTSA KUTSERO (2).
    a. Point R foot sideward right and Boy holds hat at the top with R hand and raise hat overhead (ct.1), close R foot to L and put on a hat (ct.2). Freehand (L hand) on the rear at waist level .... **(1M)**
    b. Repeat (a) .... **(1M)**
    c. Starting with the right foot, take four stamp-turn right in place (cts. 1,2,1,2) and put on hat holding with R hand. Holds hat at the top with L hand at the last count of the measure...(2M)

4. MARTSA PASAHERO (2).
    (a) Starting with R foot, stamp R, and L foot alternately, Girl holding a fan with R hand

extended sideward right (ct. 1,2). Freehand (L hand) holding skirt .... **(1M)**

(b) Repeat (a) twice ....**(2M)**

(c) Repeat (a) and bring a fan with R hand in front in fanning movement at chest level. Freehand (L hand) holding skirt (cts. 1,2) .... **(1M)**

5. PAMASADA (1).

Preparatory Movement Position. From standing position, kneel with L knee, Boy holds hat at the top with R hand and freehand (L hand) on the rear at waist level (cts 1,2). Reverse position of hands (cts. 1,2).................................. **(2M)**

(a) In left knee position, Boy holds hat with both hands in front (R hand on its top and L Hand on its brim) at chest level in driving motion .... **(4M)**

(b) With R hand holding hat at the top, extend hat sideward right (cts. 1,2,1,2), and put on a hat (cts. 1,2,1,2) .... **(4M)**

(c) Extend hat sideward right (cts. 1,2,1,2) and place hat at chest level in front (cts. 1,2,1,2) .... **(4M)**

(d) Repeat (b) .... **(4M)**

6. PAMASADA (2). Partners face each other. The Girl holds the fan with R hand in front chest level. Freehand (L hand) holding skirt. The boy holds the hat at the top with R hand and freehand (L hand) at the rear at waist level.

(a) Starting with the right foot, execute one change step to the right. Girl extends fan sideward right, while Boy extends hat sideward right (cts. 1 and 2) .... **(1M)**

(b) Repeat (a) towards the left. Partners place and hold fan and hat in front at chest level (cts. 1 and 2) …………………………………………..(1M)

(c) Repeat (a) …………………………………… (1M)

(d) Repeat (b). Girl place and hold the fan in front at chest level and Boy put on hat ………………………………………… (1M)

(e) Repeat (a) and (d)………………………….. (2M)

(f) Stamp R and L foot alternately turning right in place (cts. 1,2,1,2). Boys hands on waist and Girls holds a fan with R hand in front chest level ……………………………………… (2M)

7. PAMASADA (3). Partners face each other.

(a) Starting with the right foot, execute one Heel and Toe Polka to the right. (cts. 1,2, 1, and 2). Repeat Heel and Toe polka to the left (cts. 1,2, 1, and 2). Girl's in fanning movement while Boys hands on waist …………………………….. (4M)

(b) Starting with R foot, execute two change steps alternately right and left (cts. 1 and 2, 1 and 2). Girl's in fanning movement while Boys hands-on waist ……………………………………….. (2M)

(c) Starting with R foot, take four stamp-turn right in place (cts.1,2,1,2). Girls in fanning movement while Boys hands-on waist ………………………………………… (2M)

8. PAMASADA (4). Partners face each other.

(a) In a left knee bent kneeling position, Boys clap hands extending obliquely right while Girls execute one change step to the right. Girl extends fan sideward right (cts. 1 and 2) ………………………………………… (1M)

    (b)   Repeat (a) towards the left. Girls place and hold fan and hat in front at chest level (cts. 1 and 2) .... **(1M)**

    (c)   Repeat (a) and (b) three more times .... **(6M)**

9.   PAMARA. Partners face the audience; Boys do the entire steps in the opposite direction with the Girls. The girl holds a fan with her right hand in front at chest level and freehand holding skirt. Boys hands on waist.

    a.   Point L foot sideward left (ct.1), close L foot to the right (ct.2), Girl extend hands diagonally sideward right .... **(1M)**

    b.   Point R foot sideward right (ct.1), close R foot to the left (ct.2), Girl holding a fan with the right hand in front at chest level .... **(1M)**

    c.   Take four stamp-turn right in place (cts. 1,2,1,2), Girl holding a fan with R hand extended sideward right .... **(2M)**

10. PANIKAD (1). Partners face the audience; Boys do the entire steps in the opposite direction with the Girls.

    a.   Step L foot sideward left (ct.1), pivot to the left with L foot, and close R foot to L facing back audience (ct.2). Step R foot sideward right (ct.1), close L foot to R foot (ct.2). Girl extends hands diagonally sideward on the first measure and places hands with the fan in front at chest level in the second measure.................. **(2M)**

    b.   Place R heel in front (ct. 1), spring with R, and place L heel in front (ct.2). Girl holding a fan with the left hand in front at chest level and freehand holding skirt .... **(1M)**

c. Repeat (b) …………………………………... **(1M)**

Note: For figure (a). The boy holds the hat with both hands in front at chest level: sway hat sideward right (cts.1,2) and sway hat with sideward left (cts.1,2). For figure (b-c), raise the hat with both hands overhead.

11. PANIKAD (2). Partners face the audience, Boys moving towards the back of the Girls on the first eight measures.

   a. Place R heel in front (ct. 1), spring with R, and place L heel in front (ct.2). Girl holding a fan with the right hand in front at chest level and freehand holding skirt …………………….. **(1M)**

   b. Repeat (a) seven more times ……………. **(7M)**

   c. Starting with R foot, Girl executes Gallop step sideward left (cts. 1 and 2), place L heel sideward left (ct. and). Girl holding a fan with R hand extended sideward right and freehand holding skirt ………………………….……. **(1M)**

   d. Repeat (c) steps to the right; Girl bring a fan with the right hand in front at chest level and freehand holding skirt………………….…. **(1M)**

   e. Repeat (c-d) three more times. The opposite direction of movements of the Boys will take place in this figure……………………….…(6M)

Note: For figures (a-b), Boy holds the hat at the top with R hand and raises the hat overhead every first count of the measure. Freehand (L hand) on the rear at waist level. For figures (c-e), Put on a hat and hands on the waist. Boys will chant "Hey" in every last count of the measure while slightly bending and looking at partners at the side.

12. PANGARWAHE (1) DO-SI-DO. Partners face the audience, Girls standing halfway at the right side in front of the Boys.

(a) Boys. Step R foot forward (ct.1), step L foot close to right (ct.2), step R foot sideward right (ct.1), step L foot close to right (ct.2), step R foot backward (ct.1), step L foot close to right (ct.2), step L foot sideward left (ct.1), step R foot close to left (ct.2)............ **(4M)**

Girls. Step R foot backward (ct.1), step L foot close to right (ct.2), step L foot

sideward right (ct.1), step R foot close to left (ct.2), step R foot forward (ct.1), step L foot close to right (ct.2), step R foot sideward right (ct.1), step L foot close to right (ct.2)... **(4M)**

(b) Repeat (a) in reverse direction .... **(4M)**

(c) DO-SI-DO passing L to L shoulder.

Step R foot forward (ct.1), step L foot close to right (ct.2), step L foot sideward left (ct.1), step R foot close to left (ct.2), step R foot backward (ct.1), step L foot close to right (ct.2), step R foot sideward right (ct.1), step L foot close to right (ct.2) .... **(4M)**

(d) Repeat (c) in reverse direction .... **(4M)**

13. PANGARWAHE (2). Partners face the audience, Girls standing halfway at the right side in front of the Boys.

(a) Starting with the R foot, Girl executes Grapevine step towards the left (cts. 1,2,1, 2). Step R across L (ct.1), hop on the R foot, and L foot raise in the rear (ct. 2). Step L foot in the rear (ct.1) and hop on the L foot and R foot raise in front (ct. 2) .... **(4M)**

(b) Starting R foot, take a three-step turn right in place (cts. 1,2,1), and point L foot sideward left

and raise fan diagonally sideward right (ct. 2)
....…..… **(2M)**

(c) Repeat (b) towards the left and place fan in front at chest level ....… **(2M)**

(d) Repeat (a) - (c) ....…**(8M)**

Note: Boys do the entire steps in the opposite direction with the Girls—Boys hands on waist.

Moods: Happiness and lively

Characteristics: Friendliness, cheerfulness, religiosity, lovers of peace, and contentment

INTRODUCTION
Music Introduction.

Boys execute Martsa Kutsero (1) towards the center of the stage. Arm movements as in Pamasada (1a). In the last two measures, face the audience and put on hat holding with right hand on top and freehand (L hand) on the rear at waist level..….. **(8M)**

O O O O   O O O O

⚡ ⚡ ⚡ ⚡ ——▶ Stage ◀—— ⚡ ⚡ ⚡ ⚡

Audience

Diagram B

Figure I

Music A.

Boys. Facing the audience, execute Martsa Kutsero (1) four times, moving forward to places (8M). Execute Martsa Kutsero (2) to the right (4M) and Martsa Kutsero to the left (4M). Execute Pamasada (1) preparatory position (2M) .... **(18M)**

Girls. Facing center stage (in place), hold the fan with R hand in front with fanning movement at chest level while freehand (L hand) holding skirt. After eight measures, move towards the center of the stage and execute Martsa Pasahero (1) five times.. **(18M)**

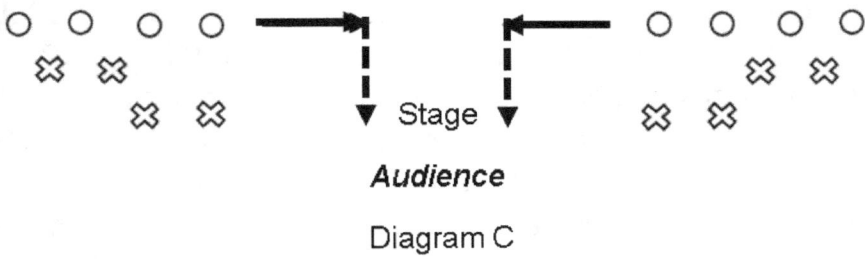

Audience

Diagram C

Figure II
Music B.

Boys. In kneeling position facing audience, execute Pamasada (1a-b). Stand up in the last measure .... **(16M)**

Girls. Facing the audience, execute Martsa Pasahero (1) four times, moving forward to places (8M). Execute Martsa Pasahero (2) moving counterclockwise to partners back facing away from the audience (4M) and moving back to places facing the audience (4M) .... **(16M)**

45

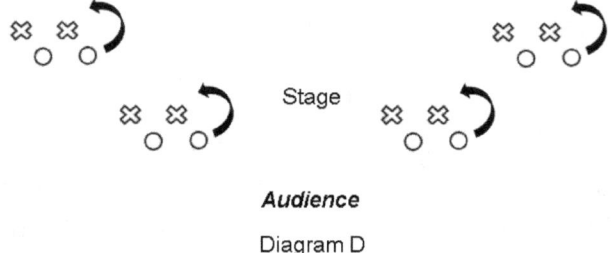

Stage

Audience

Diagram D

Figure III
Music C.

Boys. Facing the audience, starting with R foot, execute Pamara turning left (4M) and Pamara with L foot turning right (4M). Execute Panikad (1) starting R foot facing away from the audience (4M) and Panikad (1) starting L foot facing the audience (4M) .... **(16M)**

Girls. Facing the audience, starting with L foot, execute Pamara turning right (4M) and Pamara with R foot turning left facing away from the audience (4M). Execute Panikad (1) starting L foot facing the audience (4M) and Panikad (1) beginning R foot facing the audience (4M) .... **(16M)**

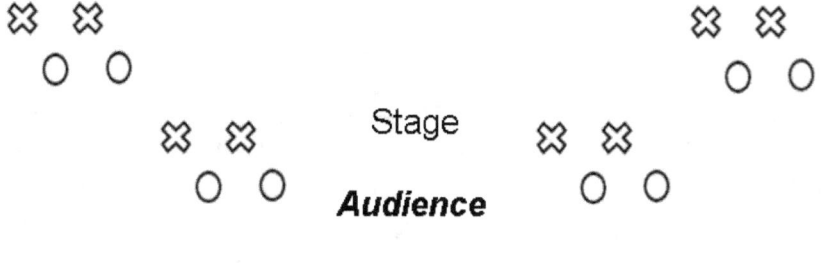

Stage

Audience

Diagram E

46

Figure IV
Music D.

Boys. Facing the audience, starting with R foot moving forward, execute Do-Si-Do (8M) and Do-Si-Do facing partner (8M) .... **(16M)**

Girls. Facing the audience, starting with R foot moving backward, execute Do-Si-Do (8M) and Do-Si-Do facing partner (8M) .... **(16M)**

Diagram F

Figure V
Music E.

Partners facing the audience, execute Panikad (2) .... **(16M)**

Diagram G

Figure VI
Music F.

    <u>Boy.</u> Facing the audience, starting with L foot, execute Pangarwahe... **(16M)**
    <u>Girl.</u> Facing the audience, starting with R foot, execute Pangarwahe .... **(16M)**

⚔ ⚔   ⚔ ⚔
O O   Stage   O O

⚔ ⚔   ⚔ ⚔
O O   O O

Audience

Diagram H

Figure VII
Music A.

    <u>Boys.</u> Facing partner, repeat Figure VII (16M). Execute Martsa Kutsero (1), hands on the waist (2M) ....**(18M)**
    <u>Girls.</u> Facing partner, repeat Figure VII (16M). Execute Martsa Pasahero (1), (2M)... **(18M)**

O ⚔   O ⚔

O ⚔   Stage   O ⚔

O ⚔   ***Audience***   O ⚔

O ⚔   O ⚔

Diagram I

Figure VIII
Music B.

<u>Boys/Girls.</u> Facing partners, execute Pamasada (3) going to partner's place passing left to left shoulder (8M). Facing partner, execute Pamasada (3) passing left to left shoulder going back to original places (8M) ..…...........….. **(16M)**

Stage

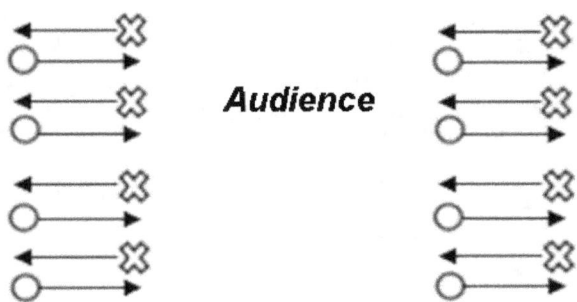

Audience

Diagram J

Figure IX
Music C.

<u>Boys.</u> Facing partners, execute Pamasada (4) (8M). Facing the audience, execute Martsa Kutsero (1) four times (8M) …………………………………………………….....….. **(16M)**

<u>Girls.</u> Facing partners.
   (a) Execute Pamasada (4) traveling around the Boys counterclockwise returning to proper places………………………………………… **(8M)**
   (b) Facing the audience, execute one change step to the right and extend R arms holding fan sideward right (cts. 1 and 2) ………………….**(1M)**
   (c) Repeat (b) to the left……………………….**(1M)**

(d) Repeat (b) and (c) three more times. Change formation as desired.............................**(6M)**

Diagram K

Figure X
Music D.

Repeat Figure III. Change formation as desired
.... **(16M)**

Figure XI
Music E.

Boys. Facing audience.

(a) Execute Martsa Kutsero (1) four times.. **(8M)**

(b) Starting R foot, step R foot forward (ct.1), step L foot close to right (ct.2), step R foot forward (ct. 1), point L toe in the rear of R foot with slightly bend knees (ct.2). Hold hat at the top with R hand and put hat at chest level......................... **(2M)**

(c) Starting with L foot, repeat (b) moving backward and end with a close step and put on hat... **(2M)**

(d) Repeat (b) and (c). Change formation as desired .... **(4M)**

<u>Girls.</u> Facing audience.

(a) Execute Martsa Pasahero (1) four times.. **(8M)**

(b) Execute one change step to the right. Extend fan sideward right (cts. 1 and 2) .... **(1M)**

(c) Repeat (a) towards the left. Place and hold the fan in front at chest level............................... **(1M)**

(d) Repeat (b) and (c) three more times. Change formations as desired .... **(6M)**

Figure XII
Music F.

Repeat Figure XI. Change formation as desired ... **(16M)**

Figure XIII
Music E.

Repeat Figure XII. Change formation as desired .. **(16M)**

Music Finale
Music F.

1. Repeat Figure XIII. Change formation as desired... **(18M)**

2. Partners face the audience; Boys do the entire steps in the opposite direction with the Girls.

(a) Step L foot sideward left (ct.1), pivot L foot turn, and close R foot to L foot facing back audience (ct.2). Step R foot sideward right (ct.1), close L foot to R foot (ct.2). Girl extend hands diagonally sideward left on the first measure and place hands with a fan in front at chest level in the second measure, while Boys sway hat sideward right with both hands on the first measure and raise hat with both hands overhead on the second measure .... **(2M)**

(b) Repeat (a) facing audience .... **(2M)**

(c) Repeat (a) and (b) three more times. Change formation as desired................................ **(6M)**

(d) End with a Saludo .... **(2M)**

ANG KUTSERO

Transcribed and Notation by Nestor A. Castaños Jr.
Arranged for Rondalla by Aldrin A.V. Ecito

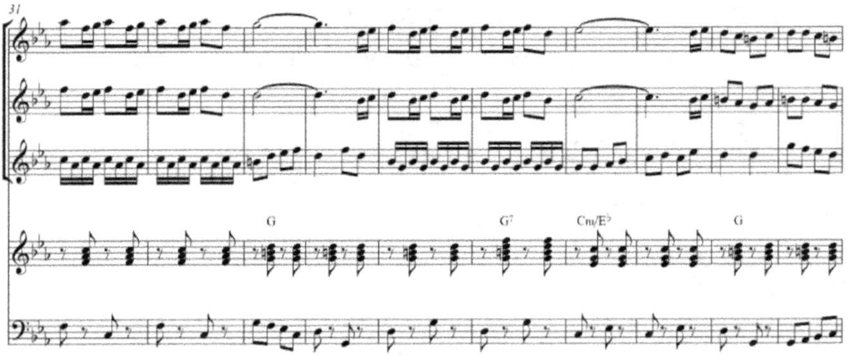

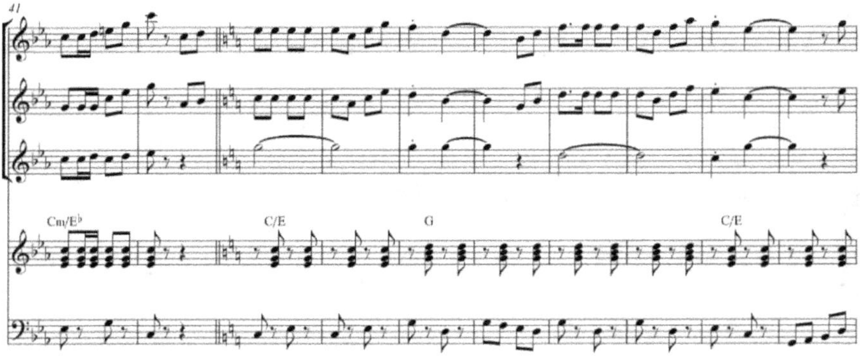

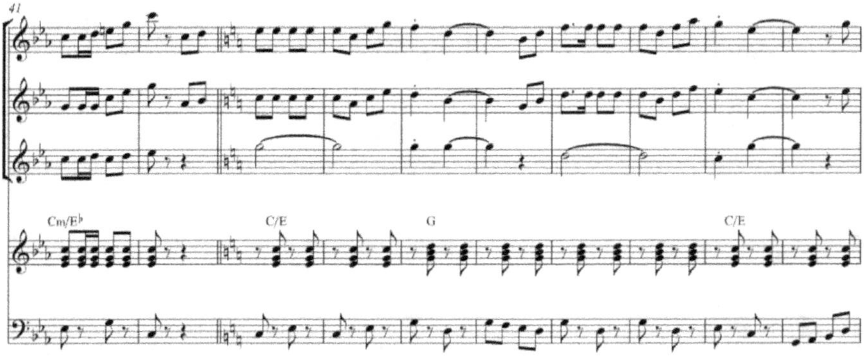

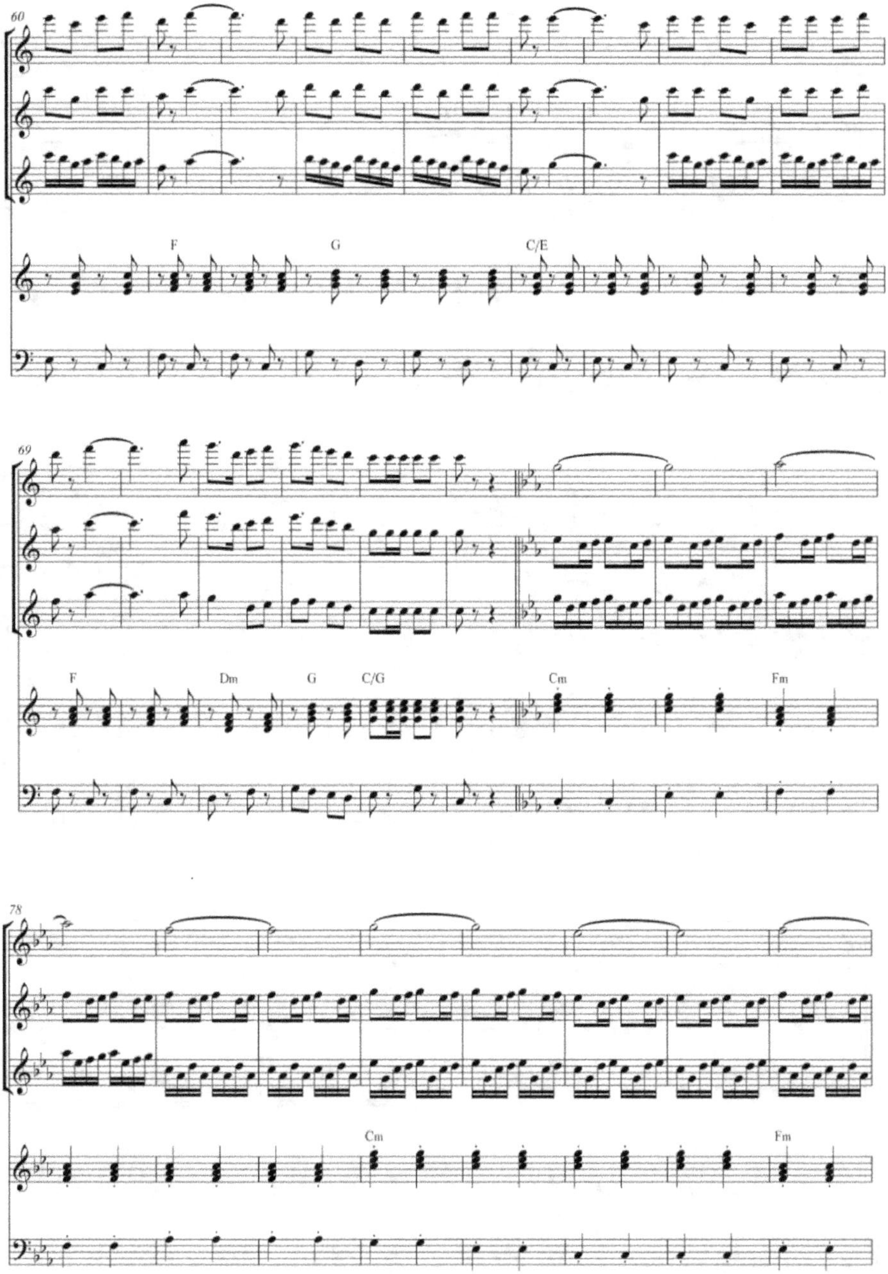
60
F
G
C/E
69
F
Dm
G
C/G
Cm
Fm
78
Cm
Fm

4

The music is in 2/4 time signature with six parts in a major scale of Bb except for part IV and VI, in C major scales. The tempo is Allegro (fast) with a beat of 120 per minute (bpm), having a rondo sonata form (A, B, C, D, E, F) which is repeated twice.

Synthesis

The study philosophy of the dance emphasizes the knowledge in a traditional type of dance. It does not just naturally occur but has a historical meaning of its existence. Ideas are acknowledged in the concept that along with the analysis of the local dance, it created a series of assumptions that focus on the development of the dance and how it was formed and comment on how the historical dance affected the culture and people of the local town of Merida. Along with the book's progress, it is ontologically described how the local dance acknowledges the intervening factors as interpreted by the local settlers of Merida, Leyte.

"Ang Kutsero" means a person who drives/manages a horse-drawn carriage known in Cebuano term as "Tartanilya." Friendliness is depicted in the girls' sweet smiles while the marching movements of dancers and the holding of the boys' hat while marching display cheerfulness while clapping hands uttering or shouting "hey" together while doing hop step jump and in the springing of foot. The bending of knees and the kneeling position symbolized religiosity among Meridanons.

Aside from being lovers of peace, the dance steps portrayed contentment as they used close-change steps, walking steps, and contraganza steps. As a festival/entertainment dance, men are performed as "kutsero" and women as "pasahero" in a happy and lively mood. The male dancers wear a Camisa de chino or Barong Tagalog and dark-colored pants with a leather-brimmed hat as props. The female dancers wear an old Balintawak and soft panuelo over their left shoulder with a fan as props. This dance has thirteen basic steps and figures, which depict Meridanons' sweet, loving and happy cultural traits before and even in modern times.

CHAPTER 7
Binaylehan

Meaning:	A localized dance version or style of pair dance during *"Bayle."*
Dance Culture:	Christian Lowland (town)
Place of Origin:	Merida Leyte
Ethno Linguistic Group:	Cebuano/Bisaya
Classification/Nature:	Courtship/Festival/Entertainmnet

Background/Content:

Bayle /bʌɪleɪ/ [Spanish: Baile], which literary means a gathering for dancing, is a popular social affair in the most barrio of Merida, Leyte, whenever fiesta is approaching for recreational or fund-raising purposes. At the earliest time, single men and women are gathered together to dance as entertainment. Men choose their partners, lead the dance floor, and dance to the beat of a sonata [sweet music]. Barrio folks have a notable version of the close-hold position while dancing; hence, the dance title, "Binaylehan," was derived.

During moonlit nights, this important gathering is considered as an avenue for most bachelors to express their love and sentiments for a lady. For a married couple, this is also one way to do away with the boredom of life after working in productive toil, by which most Meridanons seek ways and means for recreating themselves.

In some remote areas where electricity is not available, the open "baylehan" [dance area] is surrounded by petromaks' [pressurized kerosene lantern] to give light to the dance place. Like many Spanish-influence Baile, which is popular in some parts of the Philippines, this dance is performed in a quadrille (dance for four couples) whom each forms one side of a square.

Dance Properties:
Costume:

Male:	Barong Tagalog and dark karsones or dark pants for the boy; black leather shoes.
Female:	Terno in circa 1900. A long gown with butterfly sleeves with or without the stiff pañuelo for the girl; a heeled leather shoe for footwear.

Costume Illustration:

Diagram A (Starting Formation):

On a straight line formation, males are arranged at the right side of the stage, and the females are arranged at the left side of the stage

O O   O O   Stage   ⅋ ⅋ ⅋ ⅋

Audience

Note: O - Girl
⅋ - Boy

Diagram A

Music: 3 / 4 composed of three sections with six parts: I (A,B);   II (A,B); III (A,B)

Count: One, two, three to a measure

Basic Steps:

1. PAGHIMAMAT (Cross Waltz with a Curtsy/ Saludo)

    (a) Starting with the right foot, Boys execute six cross waltz right and left alternately with arms in hayon-hayon in every cts. 1,2 and raising one arm (R/L) raised to fifth/overhead (R/L) in ct. 3 of every measure ……………………………… **(6M)**

    (b) Execute curtsy for Girls with two arms extended to side and saludo for Boys with one arm extended to the right ……… **(2M)**

2. PAGPUNIT. Partners are standing side by side, Girls on the right side of the boys. Partners are holding inside hands extended to the front, Boys freehand at the waist while Girls down at the side.

(a) Starting with the right foot, execute nine dainty walks (Paso) towards proper places .... **(3M)**

(b) Partners pause in place, facing each other. Girls place both hands on Boys' shoulder blades while Boys place both hands on the Girls' waist in the rear (Gunit Pamayle) .... **(1M)**

3. BINAYLEHAN (1). Partners face each other in gunit pamayle position. Starting with R foot, Boy take eight Waltz steps. Girl do the Waltz step with the L foot ...…..……………………..……….. **(8M)**

Note: In this figure, the Boy will attempt to look up with the girl (R & L alternately), but in return, the Girl will look away (L & R alternately) with the Boy (Palingiw-lingiw). Throughout this figure, dancers are in a slightly bent position.

4. BINAYLEHAN (2). Partners are facing each other in a close ballroom position facing halfway towards the audience. Boy's L arm is extended towards the left and right hand at Girls waist in the rear. Girl's R arm is extended towards the right and left hand on Boys' right shoulder blade (Pamustura).

(a) Take six Waltz steps turning clockwise in place. Girls start the Waltz step with the R foot and Boys with the left ..…….….. **(6M)**

(b) Girls turn right in place over the L arm of the Boys (cts. 1,2,3). Reverse position of the arms (close ballroom position) facing away from the audience (cts. 1,2,3) .... **(2M)**

5. BINAYLEHAN (3). Partners are facing each other in close ballroom position (Pamustura). Girls will oppositely do the Boys' steps.

   (e) Boy's L arm is extended towards the left. Point L foot sideward left (cts. 1,2), hop with R foot and raise L (ct.3)………..………………….. **(1M)**

   (f) Starting L foot, take three steps forward (cts. 1,2,3)……………. **(1M)**

   (g) Repeat (a- b) starting with R foot away from the audience ……..... **(2M)**

   Note: In this figure, partners will do the steps in a slightly bent position while pointing the R/L foot. Boys will attempt to look up to the girl, but in return, Girls will look away with them (Pakipot).

6. BINAYLEHAN (4). Partners are facing each other in close ballroom position (Pamustura). Girls will oppositely do the Boys' steps.

   (a) Boys L arm is extended towards the left. Execute two Mazurka steps towards the audience …………. **(2M)**

   (b) Girls turn right in place over L arm of the Boys (cts. 1,2,3) ………….. **(1M)**

   (c) Reverse position of the arms (close ballroom position) facing away from the audience (cts. 1,2,3) …….... **(1M)**

7. BINAYLEHAN (5). Partners face each other in a "Gunit Pamayle" position with knees slightly bent. Partners R cheeks are touching each other.

   (a) Starting with R foot, Boys take eight Waltz steps. Girls do the Waltz step with the L foot ……..………….. **(8M)**

8. PAKIGHALUBILO. Partners face each other and join R to R hands. Boys' movements are counterclockwise while girls clockwise (Cadena).

    (a)   Passing L to L shoulder, execute cross waltz step moving forward and join L to L hands with the arms extended to the next partner (cts. 1,2,3) .... **(1M)**

    (b)   Repeat (a) to the right (R to R shoulder, R to R hands) with the next partner .... **(1M)**

    (c)   Repeat (a-b) three more times .... (6M)

Note: In this figure, partners will do the "kumustahan" while holding hands and changing partners. As much as possible, the chain (Cadena) must not break.

Moods: Happiness and gladness

Characteristics: Friendliness, cheerfulness, hospitality, family solidarity, lovers of celebration and peace, courtship and marriage, respect of authority, and novelty

INTRODUCTION
Music Introduction.

Dancers are placed and arranged on stage as illustrated in Figure a (Starting formation). In this particular part of the dance, the dancers dramatize the setting of a typical "Baylehan" scenario where the "Bayle" is about to start. While the announcer will announce to the mamaylihay (crowd) that the "sonata" is for those who had special ribbons with a particular cost, the boys will agree with each other about who they will dance to. The girls, just await with the boys until the "sonata" will be played... **(10M)**

Figure I
Music A.

<u>Boys</u>. From starting formation, facing the center stage, dancers execute "Paghimamat" towards the center of the stage (8M) with the last two measures facing the audience, and pause (7M) and bow partner (1M) .... **(16M)**
<u>Girls</u>. Pause (8M) while Boys are moving. From starting formation, facing the center stage, dancers perform the "Paghimamat" towards the center of the stage (8M), with the last 2M facing partner/away from the audience .... **(16M)**

Figure II
Music B.

<u>Girls</u>. Turning R shoulder and facing the audience, dancers execute the "Paghimamat (a)" moving forward (4M), turn R shoulder facing partner, execute "Paghimamat (a)" moving towards the partner (2M) and execute "Paghimamat (b) with the last 2M facing the audience. Pause (8M) holding skirt and facing audience .... **(16M)**

<u>Boys</u>. Pause (8M) while Girls are moving. Facing the audience, dancers execute the "Paghimamat (a)" moving forward passing partner's R shoulder (4M), turn R shoulder facing partner, perform "Paghimamat (a)" moving towards partners place standing L side of the Girls (4M) .... **(16M)**

Figure III
Music A (Music Transition).
Execute "Pagpunit" going to proper places and formation.. **(4M)**

O�֍   O�֍   O✷   O✷

Audience
Diagram B

Figure IV
Music B.
Execute "Binaylehan (1) twice. In this figure, no definite formations are required.. **(16M)**

Figure V
Music A.
Execute "Binaylehan (1)" twice. In this figure, partners will now have an eye to eye contact, attempting not to have Palingiw-lingiw this time. No definite formation is required in this figure.. **(16M)**
Note: In this figure, no definite formations and directions are required.

Figure VI
Music A.
(a) Execute "Binaylehan (2)" moving clockwise.............. **(8M)**
(b) Repeat (a) moving counterclockwise. .... **(8M)**
> _Note: In this figure, no definite formations and directions are required._

66

Figure VII
Music B.

(a) Execute "Binaylehan (3)" ……………………………….…… **(4M)**

(b) Repeat (a) three more times……………………..…… **(12M)**

Note: In this figure, no definite formations and directions are required.

Figure VIII
Music B.

(a) Execute "Binaylehan (4)" ……………………………….…… **(4M)**

(b) Repeat (a) three more times……………………….…….. **(12M)**

Note: In this figure, no definite formations and directions are required.

Figure IX
Music B.

(a) Execute "Binaylehan (5)". Partners gradually do this in clockwise movement ……………………………………….… **(8M)**

(b) Repeat (a) one more time……………..……………..……. **(8M)**

Note: In this figure, no definite formations and directions are required.

Figure X
Music B.
(a) Execute "Pakighalubilo"...................................... **(8M)**
(b) Repeat (a) going in reverse direction .... **(8M)**

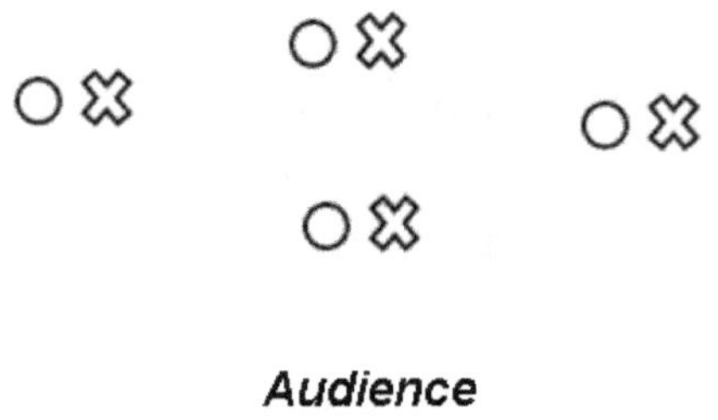

Audience
Diagram C

Figure XI
Music B.
Repeat Figure V .... **(16M)**

Figure XII
Music B.
(a) Repeat Figure VII (a) twice.................................. **(8M)**
(b) Repeat Figure VI (a) .... **(8M)**

Music Finale

Starting with the right foot, execute 12 dainty walks (Paso) towards proper places. Partners' inside arms are in Abrasiete (4M). In the last two measures, each couple may take turn in taking pauses showcasing different Binaylehan holds (2M).. **(6M)**

BINAYLEHAN

Transcribed and Notation by Nestor A. Castaños Jr.
Arranged for Rondalla by Daryll Salceda

4

The music compilation of various popular folk songs and music in 3/4 time signature is set into a medley (see attached lyrics) with three sections I, II, and III. Section I is in the key of A major in binary form (A, B). Section II is in the key of Bb major in binary form (A.B). Section III is in the key of C# major in a ternary form (A, B, B). The tempo is Allegro (fast) with a beat of 130 per minute (bpm).

SA KABUKIRAN
(An excerpt from a popular folk song lyrics used in Section I of the dance)
Sa kabukiran, layo ang kasakit
Ang kalanggaman ahay…. Nanag-awit
Maoy gaindig mga paghadla
Mga parayeg ay mga hudyaka
Ang hinuyuhoy, naglanoy lanoy
Sa kadahonan ug kabulakan, sa kadahonan, ug kabulakan
O kinabuhi lonlon kalipay
Gawas ang himili, way ikagmahay

MAGHULAT AKO
(An excerpt from a popular folk song lyrics used in Section II of the dance)
Ning takna sa kagabhi-on
Pangandoy ko ikaw kanunay kong ikauban
Ug kon kita maglagyo na
Magahulat ako Inday'ng mubalik ka

Synthesis

The dance analysis recognizes how the authenticity of the local dance can be identified along with a series of interpretations. It accepts that by the analysis and notations, the result of the book data presents an objective interpretation of conclusions of the epistemological orientation of the study results. The process of learning in the view of an epistemological position explains the historical dance formation basically from the rich culture cultivated by the native settlers. This approach concentrates on the analysis of a single process or function.

Binaylehan means a localized dance version or style of pair dancing during "Bayle" in Spanish term, which means a gathering for dancing. This dance evolved first as a courtship dance in which men choose their partners, lead the dance floor, and later become a festival/entertainment dance where notable versions of the close-hold position while dancing is displayed. Friendliness is also depicted in the dance through the dancers' shaking of hands and the girls' sweet smiles. Cheerfulness is also manifested in the hop steps, jump, and springing of foot movements, while hospitality is manifested in the arms open to the second position. Meridanons are also lovers of celebration, as manifested in the Mazurka in open ballroom position dance movement. The hands joining together in some part of the dance also manifest family solidarity. In this dance, the male dancers wear Barong Tagalog, dark trousers, and leathered shoes, while the girls wear a typical Terno in circa 1900. In this dance, eight basic steps were used in the twelve figures of the entire dance that depicts a happy mood, by which every Meridanons in the early times considered "Pamayle" as a means for recreation.

CHAPTER 8
Jota Merida

Meaning: Jota version of Merida Leyte
Dance Culture: Christian Lowland (town)
Place of Origin: Merida Leyte
Ethno Linguistic Group: Cebuano/Bisaya
Classification/Nature: Courtship/Festival/Entertainment

Background/Content:

Jota ['xota] is of Spanish origin, a music genre and the associated dance known throughout Spain. As manifested in its history, Spanish occupation in the town also influenced its customs and cultural traditions. As narrated by some old folks, the town of Merida was promulgated as a town in the year 1857 by the District Governor of the Province of Leyte named Honorable Domingo Fernandez Ember. Together with Almeria, Albuera, Villaba, and Tolosa, the name Merida was named after the towns in Spain.

Wedding is one of the biggest celebrations usually attended by both parties' kins and friends. Merry-making, eating, drinking, singing, dancing, and typically begin with the "Likod-likod" [eve before a wedding]. This is the day of parting ways: the last of bachelorhood and the beginning of marital union. Before the likodlikod, the "Pamamalaye" [a mutual promise to marry] will be done in the girl's house in a festive mood. Well attended by the parents, grandparents, relatives, and friends of the boy, they serve as the hosts furnishing the labor, materials, and other party expenses. In the course of merry-making, the spokesman for pamamalaye of the boy's parent opened the topic by reciting verses, sayings, or proposing measured language.

In most cases, the parents of the girl were also represented by a spokesman. During the "Sayod" [betrothal ceremony], the girl's parents would hand in their decision, acceptance, or refusal. Immediately after the pamamalaye, the "Pangagad" [boy to work for the girl's parents] began.

This dance is usually performed during "Likodlikod" as a formal dance accompanied by a string band commonly known before as "de kwerdas na kombo." This localized version of jota was an offshoot from the popular dance "Dela La Jota ala Jarana" in Merida, Spain.

Dance Properties:
Costume:

Female:	Elaborate Maria Clara
Top (Camisa):	Short blouse, full bell-sleeves embroidered on the edges attached to the bodice (material: starched piña, sinamay, and organza). White corpino (undergarment) comes with the Camisa
Scarf (pañuelo):	a wide rectangular piece similar to the top material folded triangularly and set over the shoulder, meeting

	at a point over the chest held by a pin or a brooch. Borders with an attached tassel or embroidered material.
Skirt (saya):	Ankle-length ruffled gown with three to five tiers. Semi ballroom skirt silhouette is cut with a moderate wide tail or kola with floral applique Sobre-falda (overskirt) with a stiff petticoat.
Accessories:	Fresh or artificial flowers on hair
Footwear:	Closed-heeled white shoes

Male: Barong Tagalog and Trousers

Top:	Barong Tagalog, long sleeves buttoned halfway, regular collar, and cuffs. The shirt front is embroidered with two panels running parallel from both sides of the chest and meet in a horizontal just a navel-line with floral designs.
Material:	Piña, sinamay, jusi, cotton and organza
Pants:	dark-colored
Prop:	Hat and two-piece handkerchief hanged freely to the waist
Footwear:	Black shoes

Costume Illustration:

Diagram A (Starting Formation):
On a straight line formation, males are arranged at the right side of the stage, and the females are set at the center of the stage

⍺ ⍺ ⍺ ⍺

Stage

O O   O   O

Audience

Note: O - Girl

⍺ - Boy

Diagram A

Music: 3 / 4 composed of five parts: A, B, C, D, and E

Count: One, two, three to a measure

Basic Steps:

1. PASO TIKOD (Walk in Heels)
   Spring R foot forward (ct.1), place L heel ahead (ct. 2,3). Spring L foot forward (ct. 1), place R heel forward (ct.2,3). Girls hold skirt and Boys arm in inverted "T" position with closed fist .... **(2M)**

2. BALSE PAGSALUDO (Waltz and Bowing)
   Starting with R foot, take two Waltz Step R & L alternately, arms in lateral position (2M). Salok to the right, L foot crossing to R with a pivot turn and turn right about, arms in fifth position (1M). Bend trunk and bow in front, arms in second position pointing R foot in front (1M) ....**(4M)**

3. BALSE PANGULITAW (Leap, Salok and Waltz Balance)
   Leap with R foot sideward (ct. 1,2,3), salok, and turn R about (cts. 1,2,3). Execute two Waltz Balance alternately R and L (ct. 1,2,3, 2,2,3). Arms in inverted "T" position during waltz balance
   .... **(4M)**

4. BINIRIG-BIRIG (Step-Brush and Turn)
   (a) Starting with R foot, take four brush steps turning R about in place. Girl's arm in fourth with R arm up, in kumintang in every first count of the measure. Boys R arm holding hat overhead while raising the hat in every first count of the action and freehand at waist.. **(4M)**

(b) Starting with L foot, take a three-step turn left in place (1M). L knee halfway bent and R toe pointing in the rear (1M). Starting with the R foot, take a three-step turn right in place (1M). R knee halfway bent and L toe pointing in rear.. **(4M)**

Moods: Happiness and gladness

Characteristics: Friendliness,   cheerfulness, religiosity,   hospitality,   family solidarity, lovers of peace, and novelty

INTRODUCTION
Music Introduction

<u>Girls.</u> Starting with R foot, take two waltz balance alternately R to L, arms in lateral position (2M). Take a 3-step turn right in place (1M). Kneel with the right knee, arms in reverse "T" position (1M)..**(4M)**

<u>Boys.</u> Pause while girls are moving. Dancers are standing, feet together (See diagram A-starting formation) while arms are in "T" position... **(4M)**

Figure I
Music A.

<u>Boys.</u>

(a) From Diagram A, execute "Paso Tikod" four times going center stage (see Diagram B). While arms are in inverted "T" position and closed fist, wrist movement is in "inward kumintang" in every first count of a measure............. **(8M)**

(b) Repeat (a) facing audience .... **(8M)**

<u>Girls.</u>

(a) While in kneeling position, dancers are in inverted arm "T" position; wrist movement is in "inward kumintang" in every first count of a measure.................................... **(8M)**

(b) In standing position, execute four waltz steps alternately R and L. Arm movements as in (a)............................. **(4M)**

(c) Execute two "Paso Tikod" to proper places. (see Diagram B) .... **(4M)**

╳   ╳   ╳   ╳

Stage

○   ○   ○   ○

Audience

Diagram B

Figure II

<u>Music A.</u>

(a) Partners face the audience. Take four waltz steps with arms in lateral alternately R and L to proper places, standing side by side (See Diagram C)............... **(4M)**

(b) Partners face each other. Execute "Balse Pagsaludo".. **(4M)**

(c) Repeat (b), bowing partners in back to back position.. **(4M)**

(d) Repeat (b), bowing to audience......................... **(4M)**

○╳   ○╳

Stage

○╳   *Audience*   ○╳

Diagram C

Figure III
Music B.

(a) Execute "Balse Pangulitaw" facing partner............**(4M)**

(b) Repeat (a) facing back to back with partner.......... **(4M)**

(c) Repeat (a).. **(4M)**

(d) Repeat (a) facing audience .... **(4M)**

Figure IV
Music B.

(a) Partners face the audience. Execute "Binirig-birig (a)" twice... **(8M)**

(b) Partners face the audience. Execute "Binirig-birig (b)" .... **(4M)**

(c) Partners face audience. Execute "Binirig-birig (a)" once... **(4M)**

Figure V
Music C.

(a) Dancers execute eight waltz steps with arms in lateral position alternately R and L to form a circle (see Diagram D).. **(8M)**

(b) Dancers execute "Paso Tikod" twice, with boys moving outside and Girls moving inside the circle (see Diagram D). Girls' arms in reverse "T" position while doing the open "inward kumintang" .... **(4M)**

(c) Repeat (b) in reverse movement direction (Boys moving inside circle and Girls moving outside circle.......... **(4M)**

(d) Repeat (b)... **(4M)**

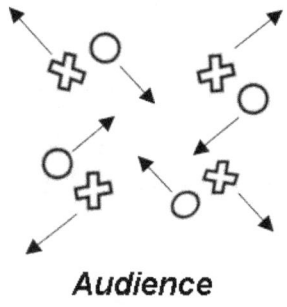

Audience

Diagram D

Figure VI
Music D.

(a) Facing the audience, execute four waltz steps with arms in lateral position alternately R and L................... **(4M)**

(b) Facing the audience, execute "Binirig-birig" turning right in place... **(4M)**

(c) Repeat (b) in reverse direction............................ **(4M)**

(d) Repeat (a) .... **(4M)**

Figure VII
Music D.

(a) Repeat Figure V (b). Boys facing away the audience and Girls facing audience.. **(4M)**

(b) Repeat (a) in reverse direction .... **(4M)**

(c) Repeat (a), Boys facing and moving right while Girls facing and moving left .... **(4M)**

(d) Repeat (c) in reverse direction .... **(4M)**

Figure VIII
Music E.

Repeat Figure II. Formation as desired........................ **(16M)**

Figure IX
Music E.

Execute "Balse Pangulitaw" four times. Formation and movement direction as desired.............................. **(16M)**

Figure X
Music E.

(a) Execute "Binirig-birig (a)," Boys facing and moving right while Girls facing left and moving left.................. **(4M)**
(b) Execute "Binirig-birig (a)," turning right in place...... **(4M)**
(c) Repeat (a) in reverse direction........................... **(4M)**
(d) Repeat (b)... **(4M)**

Figure XI
Music E.

(a) Partners face the audience. Take four waltz steps with arms in lateral alternately R and L to proper places, standing side by side (See Diagram E)............... **(4M)**
(b) Execute "Balse Pagsaludo". Girls facing the audience while Boys facing away from the audience .... **(4M)**
(c) Repeat (b), Girls facing away from the audience while Boys facing the audience.............................. **(4M)**
(d) Repeat (b), bowing to audience........................ **(4M)**

Stage

Audience
Diagram E

Figure XII
Music E.

(a) Execute "Paso Tikod" four times, Boys facing and moving right while Girls facing left and moving left.. **(8M)**

(b) Repeat (a) in reverse direction............................ **(8M)**

Figure XIII
Music E.

(a) Repeat Figure XI (a) and (b)............................... **(8M)**

(b) Facing the audience, take eight grapevine steps with arms in a lateral position. Boys starting with L foot across R and Girls R foot across the L towards proper places (see Diagram C) .... **(8M)**

Note: Arms in the lateral position should be opposite with the starting foot in the grapevine step.

Figure XIV
Music Finale

Partners stand side by side in "Abresiete" with the inside hands. Take eight walking steps turning right in place (6M). in the last two measures, execute a bow facing the audience (2M).. **(8M)**

JOTA MERIDA
Transcribed and Notation by Nestor A. Castaños Jr.
Arranged for Rondalla by Daryll Salceda

4

The music is in 3/4 time signature with five parts in a major scale of C except for part II and III, in F major scales. The tempo is Presto (very fast) with a beat of 190 per minute (bpm), having a rondo form (A, B, C, D, E). The fifth part is played six times towards the closing phrase.

Synthesis

On the axiological ground, it is believed that the dance took its rich historical background from the knowledge of the native settlers of Merida. It is thought that the interpretation of their actions plays a large role in going about the entire process of analysis, which deepens the importance of interpretation and the application during the implementation and how one wants to go in the broadest senses of understanding, at every major turn in the articulation of a new or more developed local dance of reflective equilibrium and its justificatory to be given importance in the present time to value culture through dance.

Jota Merida is the only Spanish-influenced folk dance of Merida, which is believed to be an offshoot from the popular folk dance of Merida Spain, the "Dela La Jota ala Jarana." Girls' sweet smiles depict friendliness and the holding of hats among boys while brushing the feet, and the hop steps, jumps, and springing of foot manifested cheerfulness. Religiosity can also be associated with this dance as dancers bend the trunk and knees and kneel. The frequent arms in the "T" position with palm up and arms open in the second position manifested hospitality. Frequently used movements such as kumintang inward, arms in "T" position, kumintang inward, and palms closed while partners followed each other's family solidarity. This dance first evolved as an entertainment dance since this was commonly performed during likod-likod; the four basic steps used in this dance depict courtship. In this dance, male dancers are dressed in Barong Tagalog and dark karsones with a leathered shoes and a hat as props. Female dancers are in elaborate Maria Clara.

CHAPTER 9

Pamabhas

Meaning:	A method of fishing through "Pabhas."
Dance Culture:	Christian Lowland (town)
Place of Origin:	Merida Leyte
Ethno Linguistic Group:	Cebuano/Bisaya
Classification/Nature:	Occupational/Mimetic

Background/Content:

Merida existed as a pre-Spanish village when the Spaniards settled the place. From its humble beginning, the site is situated in an area now known as Bita-ug. This place used to be a barrio of Ugmok [an old Visayan term for lowland] now Ormoc. The latter part was then named Siapon, derived from the riverbank's present name near the town. This riverbank is connected to the vast body of water (river and sea) where townsfolk could go fishing, a dominant livelihood among villagers.

"Pabhas" [Babhas, which means fish trapping] is a local term for catching fish by laying fishnet during high tide and harvesting various fishes when they are trapped inside the fishnet when the low tide comes. A school of fish may just be hiding mostly in samo [seaweeds], under big stones, or even in muddy areas where the fishnets are being laid. A variety of fish could be brought home by the villagers for food. If the catch is plenty, they sell them to people who are living in the mountains.

As entertainment, the dance is commonly performed among villagers during a bountiful catch of fish and when the full moon occurs. They gather together drinking tuba [coconut wine] with the "sumsoman" [finger-food / eat-some-food with drinks] and dance as they improvise steps without a standard routine.

This dance, in brief, is chiefly an interpretation of the accompanying popular folk song "Si Felimon" and the novelty song "Turagsoy." Both songs are also an inspiration to most fisher folks during their nightly venture into the sea. Some improvised steps are simulating the movement of a popular fish variety of the place called "Haluan" [Mudfish] and "Tambasakan" [Mudspringer].

Dance Properties:
Costume:

Male:	Plain-colored Camisa de chino or Chinese shirt, and any dark peasant pants.
Accessories:	Pukot/sikpaw (fishnet) 2 meters in length wrap around the hipline, and bugsay (wooden paddle)
Footwear:	Barefoot
Female:	Baro't Saya (peasant)
Top(Baro):	Cotton, sinamay, or flimsy material in pastel. Loose blouse,

¾ sleeves with little or no design.

Skirt: Light-colored short midi-skirt worn over a pair of regular pants of any solid material.

Tapis: any checkered/stripe dark piece of cloth

Prop: Bukag (traditional hand-woven basket with/without cover)

Footwear: barefoot

Costume Illustration:

Diagram A (Starting Formation):

On a straight line formation, males are arranged at the right side of the stage, and the females are positioned at the center of the stage

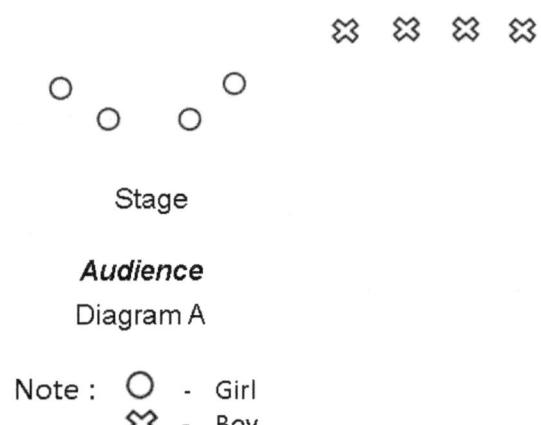

Stage

Audience

Diagram A

Note : ◯ - Girl
       �khi - Boy

Music: 2/4 composed of three sections with five parts: I (A); II (A, B);   III (A, B)

Count: One, two, to a measure

Basic Steps:

1. PAMUGSAY

   (a) Step R foot forward or sideward (ct. 1), step L close to R (ct.2). Step R foot forward or sideward (ct. 1), raise L foot across in rear of R (ct.2). Hold bugsay with L hand on the tip and R hand in the middle along with a paddling movement in every first count of each measure .... **(2M)**

   (b)   Repeat (a) to the left with the L foot. Raise bugsay with both hands overhead............................. **(2M)**

2. PANIKPAW (1)

   (a) Step R foot forward or sideward (ct. 1), step L close to R (ct.2). Step R foot forward or sideward (ct. 1), raise L foot across in rear of R (ct.2). Hold pukot with both hands in front at the shoulder and sway pukot towards the right twice in every measure............................. **(2M)**

   (b) Repeat (a) to the left with the L foot. Sway pukot towards the left twice in every measure................................. **(2M)**

3. PANIKPAW (2)

   (a) Step R foot forward or sideward (ct. 1), step L close to R (ct.2). Step R foot forward or sideward (ct. 1), raise L foot across in rear of R (ct.2). Carry bukag overhead.. **(2M)**

   (b) Repeat (a) to the left with the L foot .... **(2M)**

4. PANIKPAW (3)

   (a) Step R foot forward or sideward (ct. 1), step L close to R (ct.2). Step R foot forward or sideward (ct. 1), raise L foot across in rear of R (ct.2). Hold bukag with both hands in front at the shoulder and sway bukag towards the right in every measure... **(2M)**

   (b) Repeat (a) to the left with the L foot. Sway bukag towards the left in every measure.................................. **(2M)**

5. PINALANGOY-LANGOY

   (a) Step R foot forward or sideward (ct. 1), step L close to R (ct. and). Step R foot forward or sideward (ct. 2), raise L foot across in rear of R (ct. and). With arms in the first position, execute the waving movement of palms crossing each other in every measure. Slightly bend knees and trunk in every cts. 1,& 2 and raise in ct. and.. **(2M)**

(b) Repeat (a) to the left with the L foot. .... **(2M)**

6. PAMUNIT ISDA (1)

<u>Girls.</u> Cary the bukag/sikpaw with L hand on the left side of the waist. Take two slide steps moving sideward R, bending knees every first count of the measure while doing a "pick" movement with the R hand and putting fish inside bukag in every second count of each measure (cts. 1,2,1,2). Execute two blecking steps R and L alternately in place while holding bukag with two hands on left side waist (cts. 1,2,1,2) .... **(4M)**

<u>Boys.</u> Hands on waist.

Take two slide steps moving sideward R, bending knees every first count of the measure with a pointing movement of the R hand, and telling the partner to get the fish (cts. 1,2,1,2). Execute two blecking steps R and L alternately (cts. 1,2,1,2) .... **(4M)**

7. PAMUNIT ISDA (2)

Girls. Facing partner, holding the bukag/sikpaw with both hands in front at waist level.

Take two slide steps moving sideward L, bending knees every first count of the measure (cts. 1,2,1,2). Execute two blecking steps L and R (cts. 1,2,1,2) ……..…….. **(4M)**

Boys. Facing partner, hands on waist.

Take two slide steps moving sideward R, bending knees every first count of the measure while doing a "pick" movement with both hands and putting fish inside bukag in every second count of each measure (cts. 1,2,1,2). Execute two blecking steps R and L alternately (cts. 1,2,1,2) ……………..... **(4M)**

8. HINALWAN

(a) Leap sideward right onto R foot (ct. 1), step L across the R foot in front (ct. 2), quickly step the R foot in place (ct. 1), brush L foot (ct.2) ………………… **(2M)**

(b) Repeat (a) towards the left with the L foot……..…………………………. **(2M)**

(c) Point R foot in front across the L raising R arm with an open palm and shake waist to the right once (ct. 1,2), raise L arm with an open palm across R open palm and shake waist to the right once (ct. 1,2), shake body and bend down (ct. 1,2) and shake body and move up (ct. 1,2)…….………………………..…. **(4M)**

9. TINAMBASAKAN
- (a) (Gallop Step). Raise R (L) foot in fourth in front in preparation. Cut the L (R) backward with R (L) foot, thus displacing the L foot at the same time placing the weight of the body on the R foot (ct.1). Cut R (L) forward with L (R) foot (ct.2). Hand on waist .... **(1M)**
- (b) Repeat (a) ....….............. **(1M)**
- (c) (Parallel Tortillier). Pivot on heels and turn toes to sideward L (R) (ct.1), pivot on balls of feet, and turn heels to sideward L (R) (ct.2). Arms freely moving at the back .... **(1M)**
- (d) Repeat (c) .... **(1M)**
- (e) (Rocking Step). Step on the ball of R (L) foot in the rear of L (R) leaning a little backward (ct. 1), step L (R) foot in place (ct.2); quarter turn right and repeat the same three times more (6 cts.). Arms in reverse "T" position while doing kumintang in every count............ **(4M)**

10. PANLIBUD ISDA
- (a) Leap sideward right onto R foot (ct. 1), step L across the R foot in front (ct.2), quickly step the R foot in place (ct. 1), point L foot in front (ct.2)............ **(2M)**
- (b) Repeat (a) to the left .... **(2M)**

| **Moods:** | Happiness, tired and lively |
| **Characteristics:** | Industry, cheerfulness, lovers of peace, contentment, family solidarity, Bayanihan, and simplicity |

INTRODUCTION
Music Introduction.

Girls are formed on center stage while Boys awaits at the left side of the stage while Girls will dance (see Diagram A-Starting Formation)

(a) Facing the audience, Girls point R foot in front across the L, raising R arm in an open palm and shake waist to the right once (cts. 1,2), and pause (cts.1,2) raise L arm in open palm across R open palm and shake waist to the right once (cts. 1,2), and pause (cts. 1,2)... **(4M)**

(b) Shake body and bend down (ct. 1,2) and shake body and move up (ct. 1,2) .... **(2M)**

(c) Repeat (b) .... **(2M)**

Figure I
Music A.

Girls. Facing the audience, execute "Pinalangoy-langoy" moving in a counterclockwise direction to exit towards the right side of the stage.. (8M)

Boys. The fishnet (pukot) is wrapped around the hipline, and with a wooden paddle (bugsay), execute "Pamugsay" four times towards the center stage, moving in a counterclockwise direction (see Diagram B)..................................... **(16M)**

Stage

Audience

Diagram B

Figure II
Music A.

1. <u>Boys.</u> Repeat Figure I (Boys movement). On the last two measures, put down the wooden paddle. Any desired formation and direction may be used...................... **(16M)**

2. <u>Boys.</u> Facing audience
   (a) Wipe forehead with R hand (cts. 1,2), wipe forehead with L hand (cts. 1, 2), and hold shirt acting like its getting warm (cts. 1,2, 1,2)... **(4M)**
   (b) Untie fish net (pukot) in the hipline (2M), and unfold/open fishnet as if preparing for the fishing (2M) .... **(4M)**
   (c) Execute "Panikpaw (1)"...................................... **(4M)**
   (d) Starting with the R foot, take a three-step turn in right in place holding fishnet in front at waist level (ct. 1,2,1), point L foot to the side, and dislodge (yabyab) fishnet (ct. 2).. **(2M)**
   (e) Repeat (d) to the left with the L foot................... **(2M)**

Figure III
Music A.

<u>Boys.</u> Forming a circle
(a) Moving in a counterclockwise direction, execute "Panikpaw (1)" twice.. **(8M)**
(b) Repeat (a) in a reverse direction and finish to proper places (see Diagram C) .... **(8M)**

☒ ☒

☒ ☒

Audience

Diagram C

<u>Boys.</u> May use any desired formation and direction.

(c) Execute "Panikpaw (1)" four times……..…..…………. **(16M)**

Figure IV
<u>Music B.</u>

<u>Boys.</u> Facing audience

(a) Carry and put fishnet on the R shoulder (2M)and wooden paddle with the L shoulder (2M) ……….….…….…… **(4M)**

(b) Step R foot forward or sideward (ct. 1), step L close to R (ct.2). Step R foot forward or sideward (ct. 1), raise L foot across in rear of R (ct.2)…….……………….………… **(2M)**

(c) Repeat (b) towards the left with the L foot ……………. **(2M)**

(d) Repeat (b) and (c) to exit……….……………………. **(8M)**

<u>Girls.</u> Facing audience

From backstage, execute "Panikpaw (2)" four times to proper places (see Diagram D). In the last two measures, put down bukag in front ……………... **(16M)**

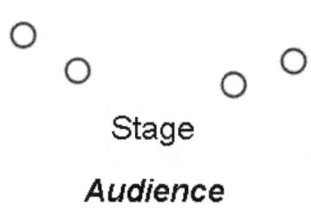

Stage

Audience

Diagram D

Figure V
Music B.

<u>Girls.</u> May use any desired formation and direction.
Facing the audience, execute "Pinalangoy-langoy" four times... **(16M)**

Figure VI
Music B.
Repeat Figure V. In the last two measures, hold bukag with both hands in front at waist level ....**(16M)**

Figure VII
Music B.
Execute "Panikpaw (3) four times to proper places (see Diagram E). In the last two measures, put the bukag down in front and pause for one measure............................... **(18M)**

O O O O

Stage

Audience

Diagram E

Figure VIII
Music A.

<u>Girls.</u> Facing the audience, execute "Tinambasakan" twice... **(16M)**

Figure IX
Music B.

Girls.

(a) Repeat Figure VII to proper places (see Diagram F)... **(16M)**

(b) Repeat (a) in place facing audience .... **(16M)**

Boys.

(a) From the backstage, execute "Panikpaw (1) connecting fishnets of other dancers moving towards proper places (see Diagram F) .... **(16M)**

(b) Facing the audience (see Diagram G), execute "Panikpaw (1)," moving counterclockwise around the partner. In the last four measures, capture partner with the fishnet at waist level... **(16M)**

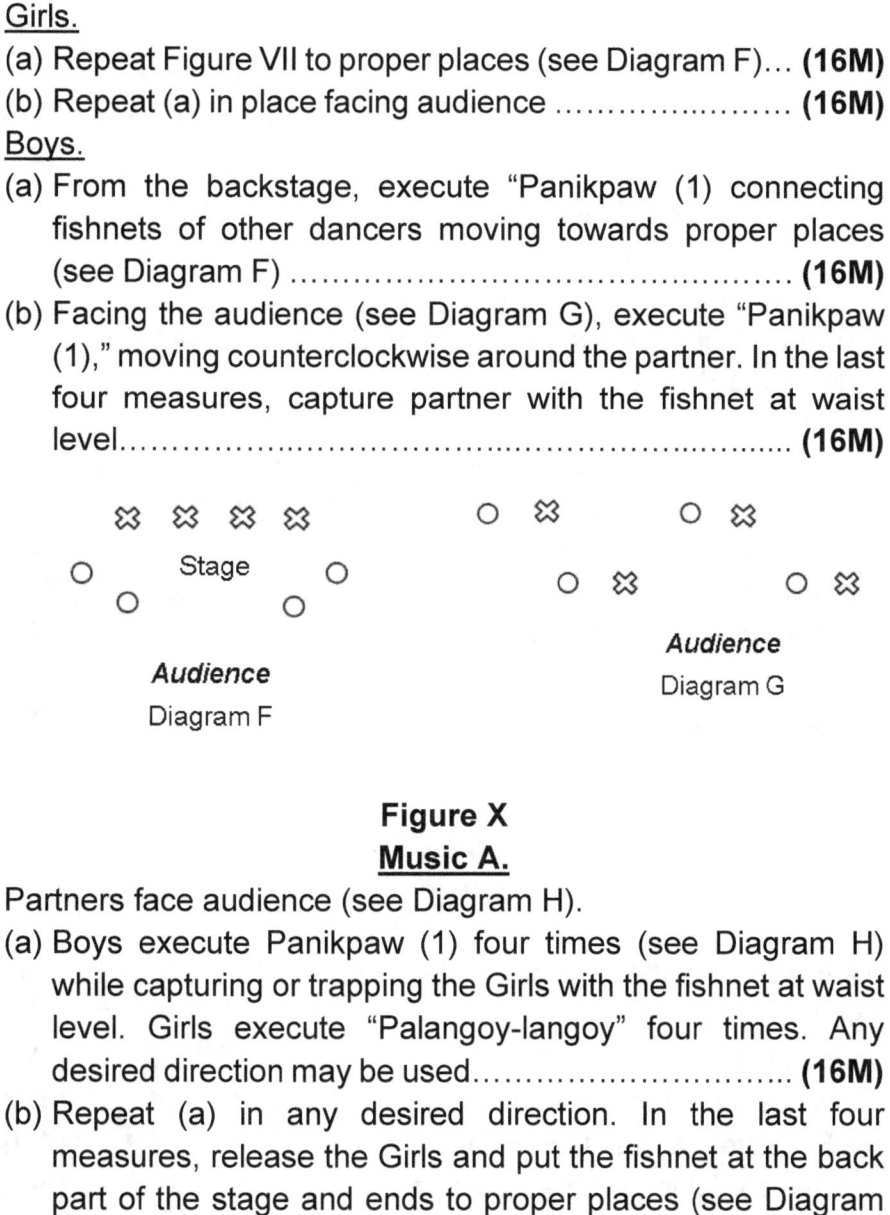

Diagram F

Diagram G

Figure X
Music A.

Partners face audience (see Diagram H).

(a) Boys execute Panikpaw (1) four times (see Diagram H) while capturing or trapping the Girls with the fishnet at waist level. Girls execute "Palangoy-langoy" four times. Any desired direction may be used............................. **(16M)**

(b) Repeat (a) in any desired direction. In the last four measures, release the Girls and put the fishnet at the back part of the stage and ends to proper places (see Diagram I)... **(16M)**

Audience

Diagram H

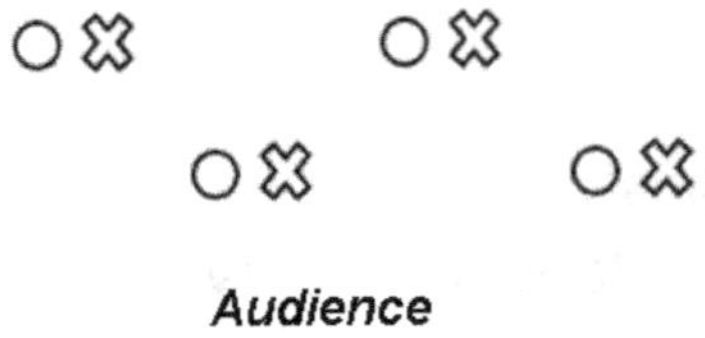

Audience

Diagram I

Figure XI
Music B.

Partners face the audience. Desired formation and direction may be used.

<u>Boys</u>.

(a) Step R foot forward or sideward (ct. 1), step L close to R (ct.2). Step R foot forward or sideward (ct. 1), raise L foot across in rear of R (ct.2). hands-on waist……………..... **(2M)**

(b) Repeat (a) to the left with the L foot ……………..……… **(2M)**

(c) Repeat (a)-(b) three more times…………....……..…... **(12M)**

<u>Girls</u>.

Execute "Palangoy-langoy" four times ……………..……… **(16M)**

Figure XII
Music B.

Partners face the audience. The desired formation may be used.

(a) Execute "Pamunit Isda (1)" ……………................……. **(4M)**

(b) Repeat (a) in reverse direction …….....……..……..…. **(4M)**

(c) Execute "Pamunit Isda (2)"……………................……. **(4M)**

(d) Repeat (c) in reverse direction……………................... **(4M)**

Figure XIII
Music B.

Partners face the audience. The desired formation may be used.

(a) Execute "Panlibud Isda (a)" four times. Boys hands on waist, while Girls carry bukag in R shoulder with R hands and free hands on skirt .... **(8M)**

(b) Repeat (a) once. In the last two measures, Girls put Bukag down in front .... **(8M)**

Figure XIV
Music A.

Desired formation and direction may be used.

Boys. Execute "Tinambasakan" four times.................. **(32M)**

Girls. Execute "Hinalwan" four times........................... **(32M)**

Music Finale.

Boys. Facing away to the audience.

(a) Step R foot forward or sideward (ct. 1), step L close to R (ct.2). Step R foot forward or sideward (ct. 1), raise L foot across in rear of R (ct.2), hands on waist..................... **(2M)**

(b) Repeat (a) towards the pukot................................. **(2M)**

(c) Get pukot and face audience................................ **(4M)**

(d) Repeat (a) to (b) going to proper places (see Diagram J) ....**(4M)**

(e) Towards the end of the music, capture or trap the Girls with the fishnet at waist level and shake fishnet as if partners will try to get out of it.. **(4M)**

Girls. Facing the audience.

(a) Hold bukag with both hands in front (2M), and execute "Panikpaw (3)" twice.. (8M)

(b) Execute "Panikpaw (3)".. (4M)

(c) Pause and carry bukag overhead................................. (2M)

(d) Towards the end of the music, shake body while carrying bukag trying to escape with the fishnet trap.............. (2M)

PAMABHAS

Transcribed and Notation by Nestor A. Castaños Jr.
Arranged for Rondalla by Daryll Salceda

4

4

The music combines various popular folk songs and music in a 2/4 time signature set into a medley (see attached lyrics) with three sections I, II, and III. Section I is in strophic form (A, A, A) with four parts, the first two parts are in the key of F major, the third part in the key of F# Major and the last part in the key of G Major. Section II is in a binary form (A, B, B, B) in a major key of G. Section III is in ternary form (A, B, A, B, B, B, A) with a key of F Major. The overall tempo is Allegro (fast) with a beat of 135 per minute (bpm).

SI FELIMON
(An excerpt from a popular folk song lyrics used in Section I of the dance)
Si Felimon, si Felimon
Namabhas sa kadagatan
Nakakuha, nakakuha ug isdang tambasakan
Gibaligya, gibaligya sa merkadong guba
Ang halin pulos kura, ang halin pulos kura
Igo lang ipanuba

SI NANAY SI TATAY
(An excerpt from a popular folk song lyrics used in Section II of the dance)

Si Nanay, si Tatay namabhas sa dagat
Pagsikpaw halwan, pagbira tambasakan

KINILAW NGA TAMBASAKAN
(Improvised version from a popular novelty song "Turagsoy")

Namabhas ko sa dakong sapa
Didto sad sa may pantalan
Tambasakan akong nasikpawan
Gihimo ko nga sumsuman

Nangabot ang mga bisita
Kabarkada ko sa inuman
Kinilaw nga Tambasakan
Among gisumsuman

Kinilaw nga Tambasakan
Insakto gayud sa kahalang
Parisan pa gayud ug ginamos
Ug Tuba nga kasimkisom

Ang sulti sa nakatilaw
"Lamia gyud" sa timplada mo
Kinilaw nga Tambasakan
Dili hilabwan

Synthesis

In a rhetoric philosophical point of view, giving one's argument a form that allows it to appeal more easily to the process of analyzing and interpreting the local dance has provided a clear viewpoint of the historical understanding of the dance giving its complete details from the actions, costumes, music and the like. Lastly, the methodological stance does the development of consistent methodology by systematizing the practice of the dance analysis process towards a continuous construction of understanding.

Pamabhas means a method of fishing through *"Pabhas,"* a local term for catching fish by laying fishnet during high tide and harvesting a variety of fish trapped inside the fishnet when the low tide comes. This dance evolved as an entertainment among villagers during a bountiful harvest. Some of the improvised movements incorporated in the dance are mimetic since dancers improvised moves for tambasakan (mudspringer) and haluan (mudfish). The dance also portrays the industry as dancers depict fishing using fish nets and wooden paddle as hand props. Uttering or shouting a weird cry "hey" together, and the frequent use of hop steps, jumping, and springing of foot while dancing suggests cheerfulness.

Movements such as close steps, change steps, touch steps, and contraganza steps manifest contentment. Family solidarity is also depicted through hand movements such as kumintang inward, arms in reverse "T" position, and joint hands following partners. Bayanihan reflects the tradition among Meridanons as depicted in the dance through portraying "pamabhas" together. This dance shows simplicity since male dancers are dressed in a typical fisherman attire (plain camesa de chino and any dark peasant pants) while girls are dressed in a peasant costume (Barot-Saya).

CHAPTER 10

Templates And Sample Forms for Cultural Dance Research

Cultural Mapping Template

	Names	Year	Researcher	Process / Steps	Feature
C. Dance					Dance Culture: Ethnolinguistic Group: Classification:

TITLE:	
Location: Keymap (See Attached)	
Resources:	
Seasons:	
	Step By Step Picture Documentation Of Process:
Materials:	Picture Of Materials:

Costume:	Picture Of Costume:
Music / Notation:	Notation Of The Music:
Prayers / Chants: None	Words Of Prayer:
Dance:	Steps Of Dance:
Vocabularies:	
Related Literature:	
Documentations Name: Affiliation: Date:	

Consent Form for Participation in a Research Study
(English)

Description of the research and your participation
You are invited to participate in a research study conducted by **MR. NESTOR A. CASTAÑOS JR.,** The purpose of this research is to analyze, record, and notate the unpublished local folk dances of Merida, Leyte to preserve them for posterity and instructional purposes. The results of this study aim to provide sources of localized resource materials for schools in folk dance.

You will be the key informant who will narrate the history of dances and how they will be performed, including the appropriate costumes and other properties.

Risks and discomforts
There are no known risks associated with this research. Because the researcher wanted only to document the unpublished folk dances of the Municipality of Merida, Leyte to promote awareness to the existence of the local dances, awareness of the richness of Meridanon's cultural heritage, thus preserved as good material in promoting appreciation and love for one's cultural heritage.

Potential benefits
This research hopes to boost the morale of the Meridanons to make them proud of their own cultural identity. The potential benefit of this research is a localized resource material for schools in folk dance.

Protection of confidentiality
Rest assured that your identity will be kept with high confidentiality.

Voluntary participation

Your participation in this research study is voluntary. You may choose not to participate, and you may withdraw your consent to participate at any time. You will not be penalized in any way should you decide not to participate or withdraw from this study.

Contact information

If you have any questions or concerns about this study or any problems arise, please contact **Mr. NESTOR A. CASTAÑOS JR.** at PALOMPON INSTITUTE OF TECHNOLOGY. Mobile number **09168778687 / 09466593500.**

Consent

I have read this consent form and have been allowed to ask questions. I give my consent to participate in this study.

_____
<Participant's Signature over Printed Name>

Date: _____
A copy of this consent form should be given to you.

133

Consent Form for Participation in a Research Study
(Cebuano)

Porma sa Pagtugot alang sa Pag-apil sa usa ka Pagtuon sa Panukiduki

Description of the research and your participation
Giimbitahan ka nga moapil sa panukiduki nga gihimo ni **MR. NESTOR A. CASTAÑOS JR.**, Ang katuyoan sa kini nga panukiduki mao ang pag-analisar, pagrekord, ug pagmarka sa wala mapatik nga lokal nga sayaw sa katawhan sa Merida, Leyte aron mapreserba kini alang sa kaliwatan ug panudlo nga katuyoan. Ang mga sangputanan sa kini nga pagtuon gitumong aron makahatag mga gigikanan sa localized nga mga materyal nga gigikanan alang sa mga eskuylahan sa natad sa sayaw sa mga tawo.

Ikaw ang hinungdanon nga impormante nga mag-asoy sa kasaysayan sa mga sayaw ug kung unsaon pagpasundayag ang mga sayaw lakip ang angayan nga mga sinina ug uban pa nga mga kabtangan niini.

Risks and discomforts
Walay kakuyaw nga naglangkob niining panukiduki. Tungod kay gusto ra sa tigdukiduki nga idokumento ang wala ma-patik nga mga sayaw sa katawhan sa munisipyo sa Merida, Leyte aron mapauswag ang pagkahibalo sa pagkaanaa sa mga lokal nga sayaw, ang pagkaamgo sa kadato sa kabilin nga kulturanhon sa Meridanon, sa ingon napreserbar ingon maayong materyal sa pagpauswag sa pagdayeg ug gugma sa usa ka tawo. panulondon sa kultura.

Potential benefits
Gihangyo niini nga panukiduki nga mapataas ang moral sa mga Meridanon aron sila mahimong mapasigarbuhon sa ilang lumad nga mga kabilin. Ang mga potensyal nga kaayohan sa kini nga panukiduki usa ka localized resource material alang sa mga eskuylahan sa natad sa sayaw sa mga tawo.

Protection of confidentiality
Makasalig ka nga ang imong pagkatawo itago sa taas nga kompidensyal.

Voluntary participation
Ang imong pag-apil niining pagtuon dili pinugsanay. Ikaw makapili kon gusto kang muapil o dili, og ikaw mahimong musibog bisan unsang orasa nga walay tulubagon bahin niini.

Contact information
Kon ug gani dunay pangutana o kabalaka niining maong pagtuon, kon dunay mga apan nga mutim-aw palihog sa pagtawag kang **Mr. NESTOR A. CASTAÑOS JR.** sa PALOMPON INSTITUTE OF TECHNOLOGY niining mga numero **09168778687 / 09466593500.**

Consent
Ako nagabasa niining maong consent form ug ako gitagaan ug higayon sa pagpangutana. Akong gihatag ang akong pagtugot sa pag-apil niining mang pagtuon.

_____
<Lagda sa Sumasalmot sa Naimprinta nga Ngalan>

Date: _____
Ang usa ka kopya sa kini nga porma sa pagtugot kinahanglan ihatag kanimo..

INTERVIEW GUIDE FOR DANCE INFORMANTS

(Local Historians, Old Settlers, Local Folk Dancers)

Establishing Rapport Questions:

Interviewer: Good morning, Ma'am/Sir. I am NESTOR A. CASTAÑOS JR., a MAED PE student of Palompon Institute of Technology currently enrolled in Thesis Writing 1. Anent to this, I am currently conducting a study entitled "PHILOSOPHICAL AND HISTO-CULTURAL PERSPECTIVES OF LOCAL FOLK DANCES."

Before we start, I would like to inform you that this study is voluntary, and I would like you to read and sign this Consent Form.

Thank you so much, Ma'am/Sir, for participating in this study.

Please tell me something about yourself?

What was your understanding, knowledge, and experience about this local folk dance _____?

Interview Proper:

Question1: As an informant, how do the dance _____ reflect the life of Meridanons?

Follow-up Questions:

Q1.1: What underlying reality can be seen in the dance?

Q1.2: Based on your knowledge and experience of the dance and looking into its movements and steps, how does it reflect the beliefs, culture, and traditions of the Meridanons?

Q1.3. What specific character traits and underlying values are depicted in the dance movements? *(Notes to the interviewer: Please check that applies)*

Friendliness	
	Sweet smiles of the girls
	Shaking of hands
	Waving of hands
Industry	
	Movements like pounding rice
	Fishing, the use of a fishing net, fish container
	The use of wooden boat paddle
Cheerfulness	
	The clicking of the castanets
	Marching movements, holding a hat
	Striking of bamboos
	Singing by the older people as the children as well as they perform the dance
	Clapping of the hands or snapping of fingers
	Uttering or shouting a weird cry "hey" together
	Use of hop step, jump, and springing of foot
	Striking of the swords
Religiosity	
	Bending of trunk and knees
	Movement of bamboo/wood from vertical to horizontal
	The nature of the dance is to drive the evil spirits
	Anointing fresh blood of pig or chicken
	Kneeling position/trunk bent forward
	Holy crucifix/presence of chapel in every barrio
	Presence of the statue of the Virgin Mary
Hospitality	
	Arms in reverse "T" position with palms up

	Serving simple snacks or lunch in case a visitor arrives
	Arms open to the second position
	Arms doing the "hapay" movement
Lovers of Celebration	
	Observing wedding ceremonies strictly, baptism and marriage are very important ceremonies
	Observing fiesta every year
	Mazurka in open ballroom position
Lovers of Peace	
	Absence of fighting movement
Contentment	
	Close step, change step, touch step, walking step, contraganza step
	Slow turning
	Slow Tempo
Family Solidarity	
	Kumintang inward
	Arms in reverse "T" position, with kumintang inward and palms closed
	Wedding dance, arms in reverse "T" position
	Hats used in the dance together in one post
	Hands joining together
	Partner following each other
	Plates, groom collects money and gives it to the bride sitting on the high knee
Close Family Ties	
	A married couple lives in the family of their parents
	Relatives are present in the match making-occasion as courtship arrangements before the wedding plans
	At the age of four, boys and girls are trained by their parents and grandfathers on how to handle

	swords the knife for self-defense and to keep them prepared in case of emergencies, such as a tribal war between their groups and other tribal groups
Respect for Elders	
	Parental consent is always secured by the children before accepting the invitation or request to dance
	Children are taught to kiss their parents' hands and other kin or made-to-do what they call "Bless."
	Bowing, children have to ask permission from their parents before dancing and respect the decisions of parents
Belief in Supernatural Beings	
	A "tambalan" or the old woman or man was known to possess supernatural powers/knowledge perform certain rituals. When an individual is seriously ill, the native believed that the sick person was possessed by evil or bad spirits. With the ritual offerings and prayers of the "tambalan," the sick are healed. If this person dies, it means that the evil spirits are very strong or the healing of the "tambalan" is weak.
	Believed in so many gods and goddesses to ask for favors. They believed that "Serena" or mermaids inhabit the deep rivers
Courtship and Marriage	
	The groom's parents give the bride a dowry or "dote" in cash, working animals, jewelry, hectares of land, house, and other goods.
	A one-day celebration before the wedding (likod-likod) by the members of the family
	Waltz step in close ballroom position, pamustura, check-to-check position, palingiw-lingiw

Bayanihan	
	Helping and working together of the village during planting of rice and corn, fishing (pamukot, panudsud, pamabhas), and transferring the house to the other place or even during their sons' wedding daughters.
	Being a hero by assisting strangers and community folks without waiting for any return or compensations
Respect for Authority	
	Allowing to deliver a speech by the highest official of the town or barrio during special occasions
	Quadrille formation, the cabeceras doing the movement first before the costados
Novelty	
	Plain walking step, passing of plates with food from one woman to another during wedding luncheon
	No required musical accompaniments to some of their dances
	Left or right arm bent in front at chest level
	Hand movement in sway balance
	Cross waltz step and arms in "Hayon-hayon"
Simplicity	
	Costumes used which is ordinary and inexpensive
	Used of inexpensive props like bamboos, castanets, mortars, pestles, use of newspaper, plates, stool, music, or sound of any kitchen utensils

Question 2: Can you tell me the cultural-perspectives or the history that relates to the dance_____?

Follow-up Questions:

Q2.1: What is your understanding of its nature and classification? *(Notes to the interviewer: Please check that applies)*

Occupational	
	Depicts actions of a particular occupation
Religious/Ceremonial	
	Associated with religion, vows, and ceremonies
Comic/Mimetic Dance	
	Depicts funny movements for entertainment and imitates movements of birds, animals, etc.
Game	
	Done with play elements
Wedding	
	Performed during wedding feasts
Courtship	
	Depicts the art of courtship
Festival	
	Suitable for special occasions
War	
	Show imagery combat

Q2.2: What is your understanding of its technical description/title? What is its implication to the entire dance?

Q2.3. What is your analysis/idea on the properties used in the dance, such as:

Q2.3.1. music?

Q2.3.2. costumes and props?

Q2.3.3. countings and number of measures?

Q2.3.4. dance steps?

Q2.3.5 moods and characteristics?

Question 3: What can you say about the entire dance?

Follow-up Questions:

Q3.1: What are your suggestions for the performance of the dance _____?

Closure:

Interviewer: Do you have anything to say that you think I could not ask you about this study?

Thank you so much for your participation. Your insights will greatly help my study in creating dance literature on the local folk dances of Merida, Leyte. Rest assured that your personal information will be treated with the utmost confidentiality.

(Mga Lokal nga Istoryador, Mga Katigulangan, Mga Lokal nga Mananayaw)

Establishing Rapport Questions:

Interviewer: Maayong buntag Ma'am/Sir. Ako si NESTOR A. CASTAÑOS JR. sa Palompon Institute of Technology nga karon nag pa-enroll sa Pagsulat sa Tesis 1. Ug tungod niini, naghimo ako karon ug usa ka pagtuon nga giulohan og "PHILOSOPHICAL AND HISTO-CULTURAL PERSPECTIVES OF LOCAL FOLK DANCES."

Sa dili pa ako magsugod sa pagpangutana, gusto ko ipahibalo kanimo nga kini nga pagtuon boluntaryo ug gusto ko nga basahon nimo ug pirmahan kini nga Porma sa Pag-uyon.

Daghang salamat Ma'am/Sir sa pag-apil niini nga pagtuon.

Palihug isulti kanako ang kabahin sa imong kaugalingon?

Unsa ang imong nasabtan, nahibal-an ug nasinatian bahin sa kining lokal nga sayaw sa mga tawo nga_____?

Interview Proper:

Question1: Isip usa ka impormante, giunsa ang sayaw nga_____ nagpakita sa kinabuhi sa mga Meridanon?

Follow-up Questions:

Q1.1: Unsang nagpahiping reyalidad ang makita sa sayaw?

Q.1.2: Pinasikad sa imong kaugalingong nahibal-an ug kasinatian sa sayaw ug pagtan-aw sa mga lihok ug lakang niini, giunsa pagpakita ang mga tinuohan, kultura ug tradisyon sa mga Meridanon?

Q.1.3: Unsang piho nga mga kinaiya sa kinaiya ug nagpahiping mga hiyas nga gihulagway sa mga lihok sa sayaw? (*Notes to the interviewer: Please check that applies*)

Pagkamahigalaon	
	Matam-is nga pahiyom sa mga babaye
	Pagkumustuhay gamit ang handshake
	Pagwagayway sa mga kamot
Industriya	
	Mga kalihukan sama sa paglubok sa humay
	Ang pagpangisda, ang paggamit sa pukot sa pangisda, pagbitbit ug sudlanan sa isda sama sa bukag o basket
	Ang paggamit sa kahoy nga bugsay sa panagat
Pagkamalipayon	
	Pag-klik sa mga castanet
	Mga lihok pangmartsa gunit ang kalo
	Pagkaratong gamit ang kawayan
	Pag-awit sa mga tigulang ingon mga bata samtang nagasayaw
	Pagpalakpak sa mga kamut o pagpitik sa mga tudlo
	Pagsulti o pagsinggit ug usa ka katingad-an nga pagtuaw nga "hey"
	Paggamit sa lakang sa paglukso, ug pag spring sa tiil
	Pagbunal sa mga espada
Pagkarelihiyoso	
	Pagyukbo
	Ang paglihok sa kawayan / kahoy gikan sa patindog ngadto sa pinahigda

	Kinaiyahan sa sayaw nga mao ang pag-abug sa mga dautang espiritu
	Pagdihog lab-as nga dugo sa baboy o manok
	pagluhod
	Balaan nga krusipiho / presensya sa kapilya sa matag baryo
	Presensya sa estatwa ni Birhen Maria

Pagkamaabiabihon

	Gamit ang " Reverse T" nga posisyon sa bukton nga binukhad ang mga palad
	Pag-alagad sa yano nga mga meryenda o paniudto kung adunay moabut nga bisita
	Bukas ang mga bukton sa ikaduhang posisyon (2nd position of arms)
	Ang pag "Hapay" nga lihok sa bukton ug kamot

Mahigugmaon sa Pagsaulog

	Pag-obserbar sa mga istrikto ug mga mahinungdanon nga mga seremonyas sa kasal ug bunyag
	Pag-obserbar sa fiesta matag tuig
	Ang pag "Mazurka" nga nakagunit sa "Open Ballroom" nga posisyon

Mahigugmaon sa Pakigdait

	Wala sa mga lihok ang lihok pakig-away

Pagkakontento

	Close step, change step, touch step, walking step, contraganza step
	Mahinay nga pagtuyok
	Hinay nga tempo

Panaghiusa sa Pamilya

	"Kumintang" nga pinasulod
	Ang mga bukton sa posisyon nga " Reverse T", nga adunay pinasulod nga "kumintang" ug ang mga palad gikumo
	Sayaw sa kasal, mga bukton sa posisyon nga " Reverse T"
	Gigamit ang mga kalo sa sayaw sa usa ka poste

	Mga kamot nga naghiusa/ nag ginunitay
	Nagsunod ang kauban sa usag usa
	Paggamit ug mga plato, ang pangasaw-onon nangolekta ug salapi ug gihatag sa pangasaw-onon nga naglingkod nga pinataas ang tuhod

Pagkasuod sa Pamilya

	Ang magtiayon nagpuyo sa pamilya sa ilang mga ginikanan
	Ang mga paryente mutambong sa sayud ug mga okasyon sama sa pagpangulitawo ug sa wala pa ang mga plano sa kasal
	Sa edad nga kwatro, ang mga bata nga lalaki ug babaye gibansay sa ilang mga ginikanan ug apohan kung unsaon pagdumala ang mga espada ug kutsilyo alang sa pagdepensa sa kaugalingon ug aron maandam sila kung adunay emerhensya, sama nga usa ka giyera sa tribo tali sa ilang mga grupo ug uban pang mga grupo sa tribu

Pagrespeto sa mga Tigulang

	Ang pagtugot sa ginikanan kanunay gisiguro sa mga bata sa dili pa dawaton ang hangyo nga mosayaw
	Ang mga bata gitudloan sa paghalok sa mga kamot sa ilang mga ginikanan ug uban pa nga paryente o gihimo nga buhaton ang gitawag nila nga "Bless"
	Ang pagyukbo, mga anak kinahanglan nga mangayo ug pagtugot gikan sa ilang mga ginikanan sa dili pa musayaw ug respetohan ang mga desisyon sa mga ginikanan

Ang Pagtuo sa mga Mahalangpit nga Binuhat

	Ang usa ka tambalan o ang tigulang babaye o lalaki nga naila nga adunay usa ka labaw sa kinaiyanhon nga gahum / kahibalo nga naghimo sa pipila nga mga ritwal. Kung ang usa ka indibidwal grabe nga nagmasakiton, ang lumad nagtoo nga ang tawong masakiton gisudlan sa mga dautan o daotang espiritu. Sa mga ritwal nga paghalad ug pag-ampo sa tambalan naayo ang mga masakiton. Kung bisan pa, namatay kini nga tawo nagpasabut kini nga ang mga dautang

	espiritu kusgan kaayo o ang pag-ayo sa "tambalan" mahuyang.
	Mituo sa daghang mga diyos ug diyosa aron mangayo ug mga pabor. Nagtoo sila nga ang serena nagpuyo sa lawom nga mga suba

Pagpanguyab ug Kaminyoon

	Ang mga ginikanan sa pamanhonon naghatag sa mga ginikanan sa pangasaw-onon ug usa ka dore o "dote" sama sa salapi, mga hayop sama sa kabaw, alahas, hektaryas nga mga yuta, balay ug uban pa.
	Usa ka adlaw nga pagsaulog sa wala pa ang kasal (likod-likod) sa mga miyembro sa pamilya
	Paglihok sa "Waltz Step" nga ang posisyon naka " open ballroom," pagpamustura, unya nagkaabot ang mga aping, ug ang mga babaye mag palingiw-lingiw

Bayanihan

	Pagtabang ug pagtinabangay sa baryo panahon sa pagtanum og humay ug mais, pangisda (pamukot, panudsud, pamabhas) ug pagbalhin sa balay sa ubang lugar o bisan sa kasal sa ilang mga anak nga lalaki ug babaye.
	Ang pagkahimong bayani pinaagi sa paghatag tabang sa mga dili kaila ug mga tawo sa komunidad nga wala maghulat ug balos o bayad

Pagtahod sa Awtoridad

	Nagtugot sa pagsulti ngadto sa labing taas nga opisyal sa lungsod o baryo sa mga espesyal nga okasyon
	Ang pagporma sa "Quadrille", ang mga cabecera ang mu lihok una, usa pa ang mga costado

Kabag-uhan (Novelty)	
	Simple nga lakang sa paglakaw, pagpasa sa mga plato nga adunay pagkaon gikan sa usa ka babaye ngadto sa usa pa samtang naniudto sa kasal
	Dili kinahanglan ang pagduyog sa musika sa pipila sa ilang mga sayaw
	Wala o tuo nga bukton gibawog sa atubangan sa lebel sa dughan
	Lihok sa kamot pinaagi sa "Sway Balance."
	Pagsayaw gamit ang "Cross Waltz" nga ang kamot naka "Hayon-Hayon"
Kayano	
	Gamit ang mga costume nga yano ug dili mahal
	Gamit nga mga barato nga "props" sama sa mga kawayan, castanet, mortar, pestle, paggamit sa mantalaan, plato, bangkito, musika o tunog sa bisan unsang kagamitan sa kusina

Question 2: Mahimo ba nimo isulti kanako ang mga panan-aw sa kultura o kasaysayan nga adunay kalabotan sa sayaw nga _____?

Follow-up Questions:

Q2.1: Unsa ang imong pagsabut sa kinaiyahan ug klasipikasyon niini? (*Notes to the interviewer: Please check that applies*)

Trabaho	
	Naglaraw sa mga aksyon sa usa ka partikular nga trabaho
Relihiyoso / Pangseremonyas	
	May kalubatan sa relihiyon, panumpa, ug seremonya
Komik / Mimetic nga Sayaw	
	Naglaraw sa mga kataw-anan nga lihok alang sa kalingawan ug gisundog ang mga lihok sa mga langgam, hayop, ug uban pa.

Dula	
	adunay mga elemento sa pagdula, kasal, gipasundayag sa panahon sa mga piyesta ug kasal
Kasal	
	Gipasundayag sa panahon sa mga piyesta sa kasal
Paghigugmaay	
	Naglaraw sa arte sa pagpanguyab
Pista	
	Angayan alang sa espesyal nga mga okasyon
Gubat	
	Ipakita ang panagsangka sa paghulagway sa imahe

Q2.2: Unsa ang imong nasabtan sa teknikal nga paghulagway / titulo niini? Unsa ang implikasyon niini sa tibuuk nga sayaw?

Q2.3. Unsa ang imong pagsusi / ideya sa mga gigamit sa sayaw sama sa:

Q2.3.1. tukar?

Q2.3.2. mga sinina ug props?

Q2.3.3. pag-ihap ug gidaghanon sa mga lakang?

Q2.3.4. lakang sa sayaw?

Q2.3.5 kahimtang ug kinaiya?

Question 3: Unsa ang masulti nimo bahin sa tibuuk nga sayaw?

Follow-up Questions:

Q3.1: Unsa ang imong mga sugyot alang sa pagsayaw sa _____?

Closure:

Interviewer: Adunay ka bay laing isulti nga sa imong hunahuna wala nako mapangutana kanimo kabahin niini nga pagtuon?

Daghang salamat sa imong pag-apil. Ang imong mga panabut makatabang kaayo sa akong pagtuon sa pagmugna sa mga lokal nga sayaw sa Merida, Leyte. Makasalig ka nga ang imong kaugalingon nga kasayuran magbabilin nga kompidensyal.

SAMPLE LETTERS

HON. ENGR. ROLANDO M. VILLASENCIO

Municipal Mayor

Merida, Leyte

Date: _____

Dear Sir:

      I am writing to you concerning our plans and proposal on the CULTURAL MAPPING of our municipality

      The tourism industry is important for its benefits and role as a commercial activity that creates demand and growth for many industries. It contributes to more economic activities and generates more employment, revenues, and plays a significant role in economic development. Indeed, boosting the cultural tourism of the municipality is one of the priority projects of your administration. Today, festivals contribute significantly to a place's cultural and economic development since they can attract visitors and create a municipality's cultural image. To be guided in planning to come up with a festival, it is necessary to conduct cultural mapping.

      Cultural mapping, also known as cultural resource mapping or cultural landscape mapping, will be conducted to identify, describe, portray, promote and plan future use of cultural assets and resources of the municipality of Merida. This is also an activity that will provide raw data and information to develop a festival in the town.

      To ensure well-coordinated Cultural Mapping activity, all clusters/schools/barangay are hereby advised to send five (5) representatives to attend a 3-Day Seminar-Workshop on Cultural Mapping. This group must include the following:
- 3 mappers/field researchers
- 1 documenter
- 1 encoder

The said seminar-workshop is scheduled on September 5-6 and October 5, 2019, at the Merida Vocational School Auditorium.

Attached is the Seminar-Workshop Proposal for your perusal.

Thank you and more power!

Sincerely yours,

....

NESTOR A. CASTAÑOS JR.

MTI, Proponent

THE BARANGAY CAPTAIN

_____

Merida, Leyte

Date: _____

Dear Maam/Sir:

     I am writing this letter to inform your good office that I will be interviewing with an identified local historian in your barangay who will serve as an informant in my research study entitled "PHILOSOPHICAL AND HISTO-CULTURAL PERSPECTIVES OF LOCAL FOLK DANCES." I am currently enrolled as a MAED PE student of Palompon Institute of Technology under Thesis Writing 1. This research aims to analyze, record, and notate Merida's unpublished local folk dances, Leyte, to preserve them for posterity and instructional purposes. The results of this study aim to provide sources of localized resource materials for schools in folk dance.

     There are no known risks associated with this research. The researcher wanted only to document the unpublished folk dances of the Municipality of Merida, Leyte, to promote awareness of the local dances' existence and the richness of Meridanon cultural heritage, thus preserved as good material in promoting appreciation and love for one's cultural heritage.

Thank you and more power!

. . . .

Sincerely yours,

NESTOR A. CASTAÑOS JR.

Researcher

TRANSCRIPTION SAMPLE

Informant: L1
Date: September 18, 2019
Time Started: 9:00am
Time Ended: 11:00am
Duration: 2 Hours
Interviewed by: Nestor A. Castaños Jr.
Transcribed by: Nestor A. Castanos Jr.
Reviewed by: Bernley Joy M. Nobleza
Location: Poblacion Merida, Leyte
Transcript No: 160

Line #	Utterances	Emergent Meanings
1	(I) Maayong buntag Ma'am/Sir. Ako si	
2	NESTOR A. CASTAÑOS JR. sa Palompon	
3	Institute of Technology nga karon nag pa-	
4	enroll sa Pagsulat sa Tesis 1. Ug tungod	
5	niini, naghimo ako karon ug usa ka pagtuon	
6	nga giulohan og "PHILOSOPHICAL AND	
7	HISTO-CULTURAL PERSPECTIVES OF	
	LOCAL FOLK DANCES."	
8	(R) Oo maayong buntag usab Sir! Maayo kay	
9	nakatuod kamo dinhi.	
10	(I) Sa dili pa ako magsugod sa	
11	pagpangutana, gusto ko ipahibalo kanimo	
12	nga kini nga pagtuon boluntaryo ug gusto ko	
13	nga basahon nimo ug pirmahan kini nga	
14	Porma sa Pag-uyon.	
	(R)	
15	(I) Daghang salamat Ma'am/Sir sa pag-apil	
16	niini nga pagtuon.	
17	(R)	
18	(I) Palihug isulti kanako ang kabahin sa	
	imong kaugalingon?	

19	*(R)*
20	(I) Unsa ang imong nasabtan, nahibal-an ug
21	nasinatian bahin sa kining lokal nga sayaw
22	sa mga tawo nga_____?
23	*(R)*
24	(I) Isip usa ka impormante, giunsa ang sayaw
25	nga_____ nagpakita sa kinabuhi sa
26	mga Meridanon?
27	*(R)*
28	(I) Unsang nagpahiping reyalidad ang makita
29	sa sayaw?
30	*(R)*
31	
32	(I) Pinasikad sa imong kaugalingong nahibal-
33	an ug kasinatian sa sayaw ug pagtan-aw sa
34	mga lihok ug lakang niini, giunsa pagpakita
35	ang mga tinuohan, kultura ug tradisyon sa
36	mga Meridanon?
37	*(R)*
38	(I) Unsang piho nga mga kinaiya sa kinaiya
39	ug nagpahiping mga hiyas nga gihulagway
40	sa mga lihok sa sayaw? *(Notes to the*
41	*interviewer: Please check that applies)*
42	*(R)*
43	(I) Mahimo ba nimo isulti kanako ang mga
44	panan-aw sa kultura o kasaysayan nga
45	adunay kalabotan sa sayaw nga
46	_____?
47	*(R)*
48	(I) Unsa ang imong pagsabut sa kinaiyahan
49	ug klasipikasyon niini? *(Notes to the*
50	*interviewer: Please check that applies)*
51	*(R)*
52	(I) Unsa ang imong nasabtan sa teknikal nga
53	paghulagway / titulo niini? Unsa ang
54	implikasyon niini sa tibuuk nga sayaw?

55	*(R)*	
56	(I) Unsa ang imong pagsusi / ideya sa mga	
57	gigamit sa sayaw sama sa tukar?	
58	*(R)*	
59	(I) Unsa ang imong pagsusi / ideya sa mga	
60	gigamit sa sayaw sama sa mga sinina ug	
61	props?	
62	*(R)*	
63	(I) Unsa ang imong pagsusi / ideya sa pag-	
64	ihap ug gidaghanon sa mga lakang?	
65	*(R)*	
66	(I) Unsa ang imong pagsusi / ideya sa lakang	
67	sa sayaw?	
68	*(R)*	
69	(I) Unsa ang imong pagsusi / ideya sa	
70	kahimtang ug kinaiya?	
71	*(R)*	
72	(I) Unsa ang masulti nimo bahin sa tibuuk	
73	nga sayaw?	
74	*(R)*	
75	(I) Unsa ang imong mga sugyot alang sa	
76	pagsayaw sa _____?	
77	*(R)*	
78	(I) Adunay ka bay laing isulti nga sa imong	
79	hunahuna wala nako mapangutana kanimo	
80	kabahin niini nga pagtuon?	
	(R)	
	(I) Daghang salamat sa imong pag-apil. Ang imong mga panabut makatabang kaayo sa akong pagtuon sa pagmugna sa mga lokal nga sayaw sa Merida, Leyte. Makasalig ka nga ang imong kaugalingon nga kasayuran magbabilin nga kompidensyal.	
	(R)	

NOTES

Chapter 1

1. Leong, S. (2013). Regional Approaches: UNESCO Arts-in-Education. *International Yearbook for Book in Arts Education 1/2013*, 137.
2. Cariaga, J. (2014). Documentation and Notation of the Traditional Dances of the Yogads of Isabela. *Authors World*, 5(4), 71-82.
3. De Leon H.S & De Leon Jr. H.H.(2014). *Textbook on the Philippine Constitution*. Rex Book Store.
4. DEM Domingo, J. P. R. Direct from the Connoisseurs: Articulating Philippine Folk Dance Documentation Practices.
5. Patrick, D. (2014). Filipino Folk Dance in the Academy: Embodied Book in the Work of Francesca Reyes Aquino, Sally Ann Ness, and Benildanze. *Asian Theatre Journal*, 399-416.
6. Ibarreta-Triunfante, J. (2021). Sense of Place of Polangui, Albay, Philippines: Identification of Its Significant Cultural Properties. *Bicol University R & D Journal*, 22(1).

Chapter 2

1. Cariaga, J. (2014). Documentation and Notation of the Traditional Dances of the Yogads of Isabela. *Authors World*, 5(4), 71-82.
2. Rodell, P. A. (2018). A syncretic culture. In *Routledge handbook of the contemporary Philippines* (pp. 321-329). Routledge.
3. AGUILAR, M. D. CULTURAL INFLUENCES OF DANCE IN PHYSICAL EDUCATION: A CALL TO PRESERVE OUR SOCIAL DANCES.
4. Villaruz, B. E. S. (2006). *Treading through: 45 years of Philippine dance*. UP Press.
5. Limen, L., Cuizon, K., Dacayana, B. C., & Vestal, A. B. E. MILLENNIAL STUDENTS'LEVEL OF AWARENESS OF CEBUANO FOLK DANCES. *BILANGAN 2*, 94.
6. Namiki, K. (2011). Hybridity and National Identity: Different Perspectives of Two National Folk Dance Companies in the Philippines. *SPECIAL ISSUE: Cultural Hybridities of the Philippines al Hybridities of the Philippines*, 73.
7. Gaerlan, B. S. (1999). In the court of the sultan: Orientalism, nationalism, and modernity in Philippine and Filipino American dance. *Journal of Asian American Studies*, 2(3), 251-287.
8. Patrick, D. (2014). Filipino Folk Dance in the Academy: Embodied Book in the Work of Francesca Reyes Aquino, Sally Ann Ness, and Benildanze. *Asian Theatre Journal*, 399-416.

Chapter 3

1. Carlson, S. I. (2019). *Deconstructing Dance Documentation: An Analysis of Methods and Organizations Devoted to Archiving Choreographed Ballet Works*. University of California, Los Angeles.
2. Hofilena, R. C. (2019). Dance in the Philippines: Various Lenses of Dance Education and Management. *Book in Dance and Physical Education, 3*(1), 47-52.
3. DEM Domingo, J. P. R. Direct from the Connoisseurs: Articulating Philippine Folk Dance Documentation Practices.
4. Jenifer, K. S., & Caroline, D. D. (2021). Rudolf Laban Techniques through Dramain a Language Class. *Annals of the Romanian Society for Cell Biology*, 3634-3637.
5. Benesh Movement Notation. (2021, July 26). In Wikipedia. https://en.wikipedia.org/wiki/Benesh_Movement_Notation
6. Eshkol-Wachman (EWMN). (2021, Agusut 28). In Wikipedia. https://en.wikipedia.org/wiki/Eshkol-Wachman_movement_notation.
7. Viray, B. L. (2015). TUBONG/PUTONG IN MARINDUQUE AS A RITUAL-DANCE OF HEALING, THANKSGIVING, AND VENERATION. *Aghamtao, 24*, 105-128.
8. Ker, Y., Chotpradit, T., O'Connor, S. J., Soon, S., Abdullah, S., Nelson, R., ... & Wright, A. (2020). Teaching the History of Modern and Contemporary Art of Southeast Asia. *Southeast of Now: Directions in Contemporary and Modern Art in Asia, 4*(1), 101-203.
9. Bautista, R. A. S. (2017). Embodied Indigeneity: Translating Tradition for the Philippine Contemporary Dance Stage. *Academia. edu. April.*
10. Johnson, C. J., & Snyder, A. F. (1999). *Securing Our Dance Heritage: Issues in the Documentation and Preservation of Dance*. Council on Library and Information Resources, 1755 Massachusetts Ave., NW, Suite 500, Washington, DC 20036.
11. White, D. R., Friedman, L., & Levinson, T. (Eds.). (1993). *Poor Dancer's Almanac: Managing Life and Work in the Performing Arts*. Duke University Press.
12. Özbilgin, M. Ö., & Mellish, L. (2018). The Cultural Development of Folk Dance Festivals and the Sustainability of Tradition.
13. Luna, K. I. F. Approaching Dance: A Book Synthesis of Dance Studies Authored by CHK Graduates.
14. Enage, N. N. (2020). The Story of a Dance Choreography of "Pasaka Festival": The Creative Process. *Solid State Technology*, 3377-3389.
15. Sturman, J. (Ed.). (2019). *The SAGE International Encyclopedia of Music and Culture*. SAGE Publications.
16. Rakočević, S. (2015). Ethnochoreology as an interdiscipline in a post-disciplinary era: A historiography of dance scholarship in Serbia. *Yearbook for Traditional Music, 47*, 27-44.

17. Storey, J. (2009). *Inventing popular culture: From folklore to globalization.* John Wiley & Sons.
18. Patrick, D. (2014). Filipino Folk Dance in the Academy: Embodied Book in the Work of Francesca Reyes Aquino, Sally Ann Ness, and Benildanze. *Asian Theatre Journal*, 399-416.

BIONOTE

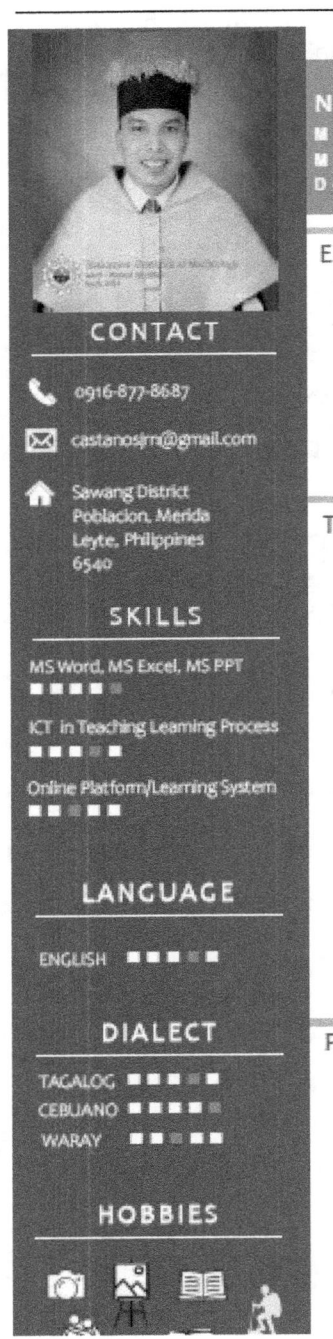

NESTOR AUNZO CASTAÑOS JR.
Master Teacher I
Merida Vocational School
Department of Education

CONTACT

📞 0916-877-8687

✉ castanosjrn@gmail.com

🏠 Sawang District
Poblacion, Merida
Leyte, Philippines
6540

SKILLS

MS Word, MS Excel, MS PPT
■ ■ ■ ■ ■

ICT in Teaching Learning Process
■ ■ ■ ■ ■

Online Platform/Learning System
■ ■ ■ ■ ■

LANGUAGE

ENGLISH ■ ■ ■ ■ ■

DIALECT

TAGALOG ■ ■ ■ ■ ■
CEBUANO ■ ■ ■ ■ ■
WARAY ■ ■ ■ ■ ■

HOBBIES

EDUCATION

Master of Arts in Education-Physical Education (2021)
Palompon Institute of Technology
Thesis: "Philosophical and Histo-Cultural Perspectives: A Contextualized Dance Literature

Bachelor in Secondary Education major in Physical Education, Health and Music (2006)
Visayas State University, VISCA Baybay City

TEACHING EXPERIENCE

Deped Merida Vocational School
2009-Present
Poblacion, Merida, Leyte

Deped Taberna National High School
2007-2009
Brgy. Taberna, Palompon, Leyte

San Lorenzo Ruiz College of Ormoc City
2007
Ormoc City, Leyte

Palompon Institute of Technology-Laboratory High School
2006-2007
Evangelista Street, Palompon, Leyte

PROFESSIONAL MEMBERSHIPS

- International Association of Physical Education & Sports (IAPES)
- Asian Society of Teachers for Research, Inc. (ASTR)
- National Council for Physical Educators of the Philippines (NCPEP), Inc.
- National Association of Physical Educators (NAPE)
- 1PhysEd.Ph
- Philippine Folk Dance Society (PFDS)/Samahang Tagapagtaguyod ng Katutubong Sayaw ng Pilipinas

NESTOR AUNZO CASTAÑOS JR.
Master Teacher I
Merida Vocational School

AWARDS RECEIVED

- Outstanding Model Demo Teacher-MAPEH (2021), Deped Region VIII
- Most Outstanding MAPEH Teacher (2017), Deped Leyte Division's PASIDUNGOG
- Outstanding Secondary Teacher (2016), DepEd Leyte Division's PASIDUNGOG

OUTSTANDING ACCOMPLISHMENTS

- Curriculum Writer in Culture and Arts Education (National Level)
- Certified National Educators Academy of the Philippines (NEAP) Region VIII Trainer in MAPEH
- Content Reviewer for Arts 5 ADM Module (Deped Region VIII)
- Curriculum Writer in MAPEH (Deped Leyte Division)
- Co-Researcher (Magmomoron, Unpublished Folk Dance of Leyte)
- Boy Scouts of the Philippines (BSP) Wood Badge Holder-2 Beads
- International Association of Physical Education and Sports (IAPES) – Head for Marketing and Advertisement
- Philippine Folk Dance Society (PFDS) Leyte Province Chapter- Vice President
- Magsanga Cultural Foundation Inc. -Vice Chair for Culture and Arts